The Haunted PLACES of Hampshire

For over all there hung a cloud of fear
A sense of mystery the spirit daunted
And said, as plain as whisper in the ear
The place is haunted.

Thomas Hood

The ruins of Warblington Castle, former home of beheaded Margaret Pole. (See page 137)

The
Haunted
of PLACES
Hampshire
IAN FOX

Ensign
PUBLICATIONS

Publisher David Graves.
Text photos. Ian Fox.
Typeset by Precinct Press.
Text repro. Wakefield Assoc., Derby.
Cover design by Design Laboratory.
Cover photo. Carl Wilson.
Location map by Jack Street.
Printed by Bell & Bain, Glasgow.

ISBN 185455 085 3

CONTENTS

The Haunted
PLACES
of Hampshire

NOTE
THIS MAP IS NOT TO SCALE

KEY

✳	HAUNTED PLACES
⊡	POPULATION CENTRES
— · —	COUNTY BOUNDARY
· · · ·	AREA BOUNDARY

1 — NORTH
2 — SOUTH WEST
3 — SOUTH EAST

VERNHAM DEAN

TIDWORTH

ANDOVER

R TEST

ROMSEY

EAST WELLOW

CHILWORTH →

BREAMORE

TOTTON →

SOUTHAMPTON

R. AVON

2

RINGWOOD

BEAULIEU

LYMINGTON

SOLE

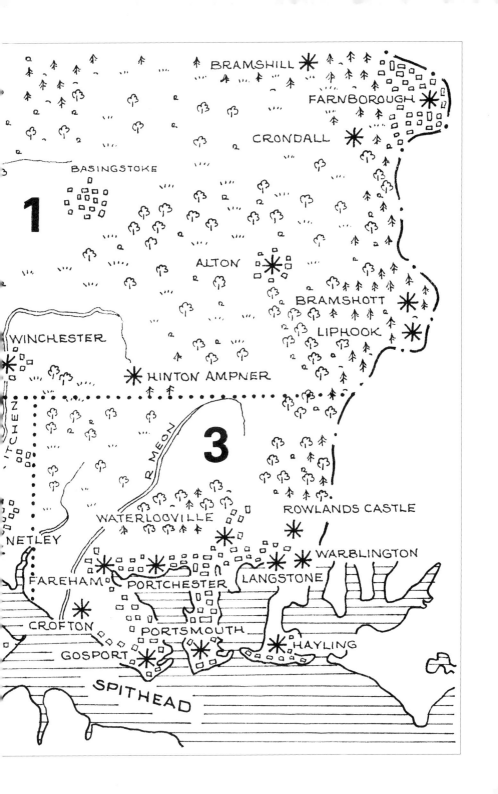

ACKNOWLEDGEMENTS

I am most grateful to all who helped in the preparation of this book. Many kind people have invited me into their haunted homes and workplaces, or have patiently answered my questions about their experiences. Some prefer to remain anonymous; they and I know who they are, and my thanks extend to them as much as to the following: Dorothy O'Beirne, David Breeze, Nick Brooks, Harley and Barbara Buckner, Jacqueline Cahill, Henry Cutting, Patricia Halahan, Edward Hulse, Carrie Kentfield, Sue King, Lord Montagu of Beaulieu, Dennis Moore, Brodie Munro, Howard Newton, John Offord, Joan Parker, Vicki Pointon, Timothy Sheppard, Winnie Sims, Philippa Stevens, Flo Thorpe, Gary Treacher-Evans, Bob Wallace and Phil Yates.

Acknowledgements are due also to the staff at the Portsmouth Registrar's office; to the librarians of the *Southern Evening Echo* for allowing me access to their files; and to staff at public libraries throughout Hampshire, whose generous assistance and advice were invaluable. ❦

THE AUTHOR

Ian Fox was born and educated in Gosport. He has lived and worked in many parts of Hampshire while serving for thirty-four years as a member of the county's police force. The author of numerous published articles and short stories, he is now a freelance writer and journalist. This is his first book. ❦

INTRODUCTION

Every era in history, every country, every culture and every period of literature has its stories of ghosts and hauntings.

Primitive expressions of belief in the supernatural and in the concept of life after death were recorded in crude drawings long before our ancestors discovered the art of writing. They were evidenced also by ancient rituals and burial customs throughout the world.

The belief is as old as humankind. And it seems to exist within all of us to a greater or lesser degree, although sometimes we may be reluctant to admit the fact. If they are honest, many professed disbelievers would at least echo the words of the Marquise du Deffand. Asked if she believed in ghosts, she replied, "No — but I am afraid of them."

Most of the people I interviewed for this book would have responded differently. Perfectly sensible, level-headed, 'ordinary' individuals, they have seen and heard things for which they can find no normal explanation. They join a formidable array of respectable witnesses, from all walks and stations of life, whose testimony over the years challenges us to open our minds.

Hampshire contains a rich diversity of haunted places, many more than can be included in this book. What it does offer is a selection of the county's most intriguing ghost stories. Some are classics of their kind; others, uncovered during my travels, are published here for the first time. I would not presume to be judgemental about them, neither am I qualified to explore their mystery scientifically. And when I say that a ghost haunts a particular place, usually it is to avoid the tediously repetitive use of 'reputedly'.

Certainly I have been surprised to encounter an almost total lack of ridicule during my researches. Most people had a story to tell, however insignificant, either from their own experience or from what others had told them. I discovered a general acceptance that 'there must be something in it'. The ancient beliefs persist — but they are increasingly supported by a considerable weight of evidence.

Bramshill House, now the Police Staff College, is Hampshire's most haunted house. (See Bramshill)

Science has a habit of burying its head in the sand when it comes across something which it cannot explain logically. To the sceptics I can say only this. Here are the facts presented to me by sincere, intelligent people or as recorded in contemporary accounts and in Hampshire folklore. You must form your own conclusions.

Ian Fox

December, 1992

Section One
THE NORTH

The re-enactment of historic battles is not the prerogative of those groups of costumed enthusiasts with their mock cannon and reproduction pikes. Sometimes the conflict is fought again and again by the very soldiers who experienced fear, bloodshed and violent death on the battlefield.

They are the phantom armies, men once involved in events so traumatic that their spirits are forever drawn back to the scene. Occult echoes of such great battles as Naseby, Culloden, Edgehill and Marston Moor have been seen and heard repeatedly by numerous witnesses over the years.

An historic Alton church felt the heat and clamour of battle during the Civil War. Parts of St Lawrence's date from around 1070; Norman craftsmen probably made the naive carvings on the pillars at the base of its tower, including a cock, a kicking donkey and a wolf gnawing on a bone. But deep bullet holes in the wooden front door are reminders of a more turbulent moment in the church's long history.

Parliamentarian troops under Sir William Waller attacked Alton, a Royalist stronghold, in December 1643. When their cavalry fled, five-hundred of the King's foot-soldiers were left facing Waller's men. The survivors fell back into St Lawrence's church, defending it for upwards of six hours before the Cromwellians forced an entry to engage in hand-to-hand fighting within its walls. Royalist Colonel Richard Boles made his valiant last stand in the pulpit: his memorial in Winchester Cathedral records how he 'slew with his sword six or seven of them and then was slayne himself, with sixty of his men about him'.

Is it possible for the terror and tumult of that bloody day to be etched somehow into the very fabric, the memory as it were, of the church? Or do ghostly Royalists return to fight again with the Roundhead enemy? Historian Dorothea St Hill Bourne, herself a keen recorder of the supernatural, has told of an evening when she attended service in St Lawrence's and suddenly seemed to

St Lawrence's Church, Alton, where phantom soldiers still fight a Civil War battle.

sense, all around her, the presence of a desperate band of fighting soldiers.

An Alton man assured her that he knew at least six other people who on other occasions had also had the uncanny impression of a great clash of arms within the church, even actually hearing the echoes of conflict, as if the battle still raged about them.

Peter Underwood, President of The Ghost Club, tells of another strange phenomenon at the church. Visitors entering the porch occasionally discern a strong perfume of lily-of-the-valley, an overpowering scent experienced even out of season. A scholarly man, one of a group of five people who all remarked on it in 1971, told Underwood how he made a thorough but fruitless search for its origin, finally confessing himself "completely baffled". Such inexplicable floral perfumes are not uncommon (they are often reported, for example, at haunted Bramshill House), and the absence of any logical explanation inevitably invites consideration of unearthly causes.

The Crown Hotel is just down the road from the church, on a site where an inn has stood since at least 1666. There is a legend (again typical of so many others) that the two buildings were once linked by a secret tunnel. Certainly the Crown holds many mysteries. Current landlords Harley and Barbara Buckner have found bricked-up passageways, hidden rooms and even a long-forgotten flight of stairs.

Many of the timbers, they told me, were stripped from old warships in Hampshire's dockyards, and it is said that if you put your ear to the posts when storm winds blow up from the sea, you can hear the cries of sailors and the wind howling through the rigging.

More than one ghost haunts this old inn. Most celebrated is the phantom dog which for many years was heard whimpering and scratching but never seen. The story is told of its cruel, drunken owner who killed the unfortunate animal by smashing it against a chimney-breast which can still be seen in the dining-room. Two Pekinese belonging to a former landlord reportedly behaved in a frantic manner whenever they were near that fireplace.

Workmen carrying out alterations in 1967 made a significant discovery when they cleared away a false wall near the fireplace. Behind the wall lay the skeleton of a dog. Nobody knows how it came to be there, but even after its removal the hauntings continue.

One morning, probably in 1985, Harley Buckner came downstairs with a barmaid to lay the dining-room for breakfast and found distinct impressions of a dog's paws on the bar top, as though an animal had rested its forepaws there. "It was hardly conceivable that our own dog, Max, could have been responsible," he told me. "He had no access to that area then." A barman found similar, equally inexplicable paw impressions on another occasion.

A live-in barman fled when he actually encountered the ghostly dog. Unaware that he had taken employment at a haunted inn, the man assumed the black dog that he passed as he came into the dining-room early one morning was Max, the Buckners' pet. But then he immediately found Max behind the bar. The barman reported the mystery after making an unsuccessful search of the locked building for the other animal, becoming so terrified when he learned about the ghost that he packed his bags, left the hotel and could not be persuaded to return.

A phantom woman also haunts the Crown. According to some accounts she is a former serving wench or maidservant, an ethereal being more often

A ghostly dog has been heard in the Crown Hotel, a former coaching inn.

sensed than seen for many years. Mrs Buckner felt her presence recently while sitting up late at night, counting the day's takings. "I knew that I was alone downstairs," she told me, "but I definitely experienced the strangest feeling, as if somebody had just walked past me."

One of the barmaids was sitting quietly with other staff members at 11.30 another night when she shivered, exclaiming in astonishment, "Someone's just brushed my hair!" And a previous manager saw the shadowy figure of a woman pass the door of his office at about 9.00 am. No one was there when he rushed out.

One legend about the Crown seems debatable. Although it is claimed that the murder of Fanny Adams in 1867 was planned there, Frederick Baker's dreadful crime was more likely to have been unpremeditated. He butchered the eight-year-old at a spot later enclosed in the Amery Hill school playing field, and while I was researching her story for a magazine a few years ago a number of

Edmund Spenser's ghost haunts the area around his former home in Amery Street.

locals assured me that the child's pathetic ghost still wanders the vicinity. However, none of them was able to quote any recent sightings.

In another part of Alton, a plaque on a house in hilly Amery Street commemorates that in 1590 it was the home of Edmund Spenser, the poet who found favour by being the first to call Elizabeth I 'Gloriana' and dedicating to her his masterpiece *The Faerie Queen*. He seems to be drawn back to his former home. Peter Underwood tells of a ghostly little man occasionally seen in this area, a short-haired figure wearing the costume of Elizabethan times, who is believed to be Spenser's phantom. ❦

BRAMSHILL

If you wish to find Hampshire's most haunted house, take the Reading road from Hartley Wintney for about two miles before turning right down a narrow lane. It leads through an old gatehouse to a straight mile-long drive flanked by a park stocked with white deer. Bramshill House stands majestically at the end of the drive, protected by an impressive array of electronic alarms, television cameras and security guards. For nowadays Bramshill is the home of the Police Staff College.

Senior police officers from many parts of the world attend courses here, sharing the magnificent seventeenth-century building with at least eleven ghosts. And what a mixed bunch of phantoms they are! Top of the list comes the White Lady, followed closely by a family group — Grey Lady, husband and son. The boy never appears, but marks his invisible presence by crying bitterly in the cellar.

A woman dressed in Stuart costume and a nun have been seen on separate occasions in the Roman Catholic chapel. The grounds are haunted by a little green man, a drowned gardener and a deerkeeper, while the wraiths of a bearded man and a twentieth-century tennis player have appeared inside the house.

Each has some connection with Bramshill's long history. The present mansion, considered to be one of the nation's finest Jacobean treasures, was built between 1605 and 1612 by Lord Zouche on the site of an older building which he demolished. Of the original fortified house owned by Sir John Foxley early in the fourteenth century, Zouche retained only part of the cellars and an imposing vaulted entrance still known as the Foxley Gate. But there was a manor at Bramshill (or 'broom-hill') long before Foxley's day, even before the arrival of the Conqueror.

A massive tree known as the Keeper's Oak stands just outside the walled garden, a slowly-rotting giant so old that great supports bear the weight of its boughs. Near this spot George Abbott, Archbishop of Canterbury, accidentally (or carelessly) shot a keeper with a crossbow bolt in 1621 while hunting deer as Zouche's guest.

Ghosts appear near the Mistletoe Bough Chest in Bramshill's reception hall

Peter Hawkins died of his wound and the Archbishop found himself forever disgraced by his tragic error, even though he paid Hawkins' widow a pension of £20 and did a penance every week for the rest of his life. Over the years there have been reports of the keeper's ghost having been seen near the tree, in the area where he received his fatal injury.

The beautiful rose-brick mansion passed through several hands after Zouche's death in 1625, until Sir John Cope acquired it in 1699. His family was to hold Bramshill for nearly 240 years. The second Lord Brocket was its last private owner, from 1935 until its sale in 1953 to the Home Office.

Despite its busy modern life as the focal point for senior police training, Bramshill House retains a timeless, serene atmosphere. Late in the evening, when staff and students have retired and peace settles over the old building, it is easy to imagine the ghosts stirring within its walls. Perhaps the security guard on duty in the darkened reception hall glances nervously at an ornate Italian chest opposite the main door, expecting to see a sad-faced woman hovering nearby. For this is believed to be the fabled Mistletoe Bough Chest in which a young bride met a horrible death.

According to legend, she found the chest in a remote room and successfully hid in it while playing hide-and-seek during her Christmas wedding celebrations. Unable to operate its spring catch from inside, she was entombed for fifty years until a housekeeper found her corpse, still in its wedding gown and clutching a sprig of mistletoe.

Other Hampshire houses, notably Marwell Hall near Winchester, have laid claim to the Mistletoe Bough Chest legend over the years, and it has to be said that it is well-known on the continent too. Another old wedding chest which remained at Bramshill until 1812 was also reputed to be that associated with the story. To muddy the waters even further, some authorities say the tragedy actually happened in Italy, where the child-bride Genevre Orsini died in identical circumstances in 1727. They suggest that the fifth Baronet Cope brought the present chest back from his travels in Italy — along with poor Genevre's ghost.

But whatever the truth, and whether or not she has any connection with the legend, a sad-faced phantom woman has haunted Bramshill for years. She seems to favour the spectacular Long Gallery, the area around the chest and the small Fleur de Lys room, now the college librarian's office. Some who have seen her claim that she is dressed in white, others that she wears grey. Or are there in fact two separate ghosts?

A security guard described his experience in 1982. "I was alone in the reception hall when suddenly there was a gust of air and the shadowy image of a lady in a white shroud or robe appeared. She disappeared through the wall over the old chest."

Another night guard saw her standing by the chest in 1985, after a floral perfume suddenly filled the air. "She was a young woman dressed in a long white gown and surrounded by an air of great sadness," he said. This man watched the semi-solid phantom for over a minute before it faded away.

Some fifty years earlier Joan Penelope Cope related in her childhood memoirs how she and her brother Anthony often awoke to find a spectral young woman in their bedrooms, usually at about three o'clock in the morning. The phantom wore a completely plain, sleeveless robe. Her eyes 'seemed to swallow up the rest of her entirely — not that they were extra big, but they were black with a kind of dead light in them'. She appeared particularly sad on one occasion, with downcast eyes, dishevelled hair and what appeared to be tears rolling down her cheeks.

The ghostly lady also visited Penelope Cope's mother. When she married into the family Mrs Cope had been assured that all tales of the Bramshill hauntings were without foundation, but her complacency was shattered one day as she lay ill in bed. First she heard an inexplicable noise like heavy, spurred boots running up the stairs. Within minutes the stifling scent of lilies filled her bedroom and the figure of a once-beautiful woman dressed in a 'pale grey' dress appeared, almost leaning over the bed.

Long before that incident, Penelope Cope's great-grandfather, Sir William Cope, was standing on the terrace with other members of the family when they saw what they took to be a housemaid in her nightdress leaning over a balustrade at the other end of the terrace. The butler, ordered by Sir William to go and remonstrate with the girl, was astonished when the figure leaped over the balustrade and simply vanished.

A young Hampshire police constable never forgot the day when the apparition of a woman suddenly materialised through a wall in the mansion, gliding silently past him to disappear into the opposite wall. Previously unaware that Bramshill was haunted, he was even more surprised not long afterwards to read an account by a Reading woman who had witnessed precisely the same thing while working there as a Red Cross volunteer.

The phantom woman has even appeared to royalty. King Michael of Rumania, whose family occupied part of the mansion from 1950 to 1952, asked for his two children to be moved because a young woman walked through their bedroom while they were in bed. Shortly afterwards his queen was surprised to find a 'beautiful young lady' sitting in the King's chair by the television. When she looked again the figure had soundlessly disappeared. The description given by the Queen tallied with that of Bramshill's celebrated ghost.

Then there was the footman who reported that 'a lovely young lady in an old grey costume' persistently walked through his bedroom. He actually jumped from his bed and tried to grasp her one night but the apparition dissolved in his arms, leaving a heavy floral perfume behind.

The ghostly perfume of lily-of-the-valley was discerned on this staircase.

This inexplicable, almost stifling, fragrance remains the most persistently reported phenomenon at Bramshill. Even in winter, when flowers are not in bloom, staff and visitors constantly report smelling arum lilies or lily-of-the-valley in the mansion, often accompanied by a sharp drop in temperature. Such obvious explanations as after-shave or perfume have been investigated and discounted. I last visited Bramshill on a November day in 1991, to be told by a receptionist that she had noticed the scent the previous day, at the foot of the winding stairs leading to the haunted Long Gallery.

It was there that Fred Cook smelled the perfume after seeing the ghost just once during the forty years he worked at Bramshill. He had heard the tales from other members of staff, and from the King and Queen of Rumania, but not until he checked the house with his dog at twilight one day did he share their experience.

As he opened the door of the Long Gallery he saw the Grey Lady staring at him. His Labrador 'gave one howl of terror and fell over backwards' before bolting for home, followed closely by Fred Cook. And when he returned apprehensively to the Long Gallery all that remained of the ghostly presence was the scent of lilies.

PC Dennis Moore, a practical, level-headed policeman and former sceptic, had been twelve years at Bramshill when he told me about the day he smelled the ghostly perfume. "It was late November," he recalled. "I was with a small group in an office at the top of the Queen Anne staircase when this beautiful smell, similar to lily-of-the-valley, wafted in. I watched the faces of the other people who in turn also took deep sniffs. One of the secretaries just looked at me and said, 'She's here'. I experienced a feeling of peace and tranquillity, just as though a weight had gone off my shoulders. It was beautiful."

It is a perception shared by most who smell the unusual fragrance. A young woman clerk who often found it suddenly surrounding her desk said in 1980, "It's a lovely smell, very heavy and relaxing and not at all frightening." Two of her colleagues also commented on the smell that seemed to move from one part of their office to another, as though a person was walking about. One described it as 'pleasant, fresh and strong', while the other made the point: "It's not like any perfume that girls wear these days. It is a very old-fashioned smell."

Little is known about two male ghosts who share the mansion's panelled corridors and quiet rooms with the phantom lady (or ladies). There is an unsubstantiated story that the Grey Lady's husband was tried and executed at Bramshill early in the seventeenth century for some unspecified crime. His 'presence' has long been felt in what is now known as the high administration corridor and in three rooms leading off it, and in 1987 a medium collaborating on a Canadian television production about Bramshill's ghosts claimed to have contacted his spirit in the stable block.

Another wraith, seen staring in through a hall window and also in the area around the old chest, is said to resemble an old man with a long beard. Nobody knows who he is, but the sightings near the chest (some witnesses report him actually leaning over it) have prompted suggestions that he could be the entombed bride's father or husband.

A more modern phantom startled a security guard by walking from outside into the reception hall, not through a door but through part of the wall where a door used to be sited. Dressed for a game of tennis, the apparition crossed the hall to disappear through the opposite wall. Those who investigated this sighting found that he bore a resemblance to the son of a previous owner of Bramshill, a young man who died tragically after falling from a train at Surbiton during the 1930s.

Then there is Joan Penelope Cope's remarkable story of the Green Man.

Her parents were puzzled by the child's constant, excited references to a green man who only appeared near water. She saw him while being pushed in her pram near the big lake, while being bathed and sometimes near large puddles, a figure invisible to adults who were with her. All they could get from the little girl was that the green figure 'looks like Daddy . . . got no legs'. A green man with no legs? The family put it down to childish fantasy.

Not until many years later did they learn about their eccentric ancestor Henry Cope, friend of George III, who had caused quite a stir in Brighton early in the nineteenth century through his curious predilection for the colour green. Dubbed 'The Green Man' by the bemused locals, he ate nothing but greens, dressed in green and furnished his green rooms with green furniture. Green-liveried horses pulled his green gig.

Henry Cope went completely insane in 1806, twice flinging himself from the cliffs onto Brighton beach; his second suicide attempt was successful. Does the tortured spirit of this strange man, killed near the sea, find itself attracted still to water? Curiously, there is a room at Bramshill where in the middle of this century white enamelling was removed to reveal stylized impressions of green plants and flowers covering the panelled walls. And as for the ghostly figure apparently having no legs — Henry Cope could not obtain green knee-length boots, so his were black.

There seems no end to the supernatural happenings at Bramshill. A whole host of phantoms was once seen floating some two feet in the air in the Chapel Drawing Room, where researchers found that the floor had at some time been lowered during alterations.

A spectral woman in Queen Anne clothing has also appeared there, holding her skirts up in front as she glided regally across the floor. A titled visitor was moved to tears in the same room when a great feeling of sadness overcame her as a small, invisible hand slipped into hers.

On my last visit I learned of the night patrol guards who, on two separate occasions, felt restraining hands on their shoulders as they went to push against a door leading onto the roof and a small balustrade. Each time the door was insecure. And a police chief superintendent told me of a windless day in 1989 when, as he sat with students on the terrace, a heavy iron gate slowly opened and closed itself, as if someone had passed through. They even saw the latch lift and drop. That evening the commandant's wife — who lived in the mansion — told

The Chapel Drawing Room, where a crowd of phantoms walked above the floor.

them that at precisely the same time one of the doors in the Bow Room had slowly opened and she had suddenly felt remarkably cold.

College librarian Sue King, who has her office in the haunted Fleur de Lys room, told me that she has had no ghostly encounters — unlike two senior civil servants occupying nearby offices. One, she recalled, left hurriedly when an icy atmosphere invaded his centrally-heated room. The other also packed-up for the day as wind whistled unaccountably through his draught-proof office, slamming shut a window. Mrs King also told me of a visitor who reported hearing the sound of a child crying in an unoccupied room off the same corridor.

The strange happenings at Bramshill, experienced over many years and by so many reputable, level-headed people, defy rational explanation. But at least the ghosts are friendly, with one possible exception. Several people have reported feeling sheer terror in certain areas around the big lake, where dogs have cringed, cowered and bolted in fright at something unseen. They may have sensed the presence of Bramshill's only malevolent spirit, the ghost of a gardener who drowned in the lake many years ago.

BRAMSHOTT

Sunlight scarcely penetrates some of the winding, sunken lanes around Bramshott. Walking or riding through the silent gloom beneath overhanging trees, hemmed in by banks far above head height, travellers in bygone times must have dreaded meeting one of the many ghosts for which the area is renowned. Bramshott boasts more spooks than any other village in England.

Typical of the old tales is that of a horseman who suddenly heard music coming, he fancied, from the top of a tree as he rode homewards at the turn of the century. Some accounts say the sweet music came from a flute, others that it was from Pan pipes.

Then he became aware of a fair-haired boy walking just in front of his horse, playing the instrument. The rider trotted his mount forwards but before he could speak to the lad an overhanging bramble tipped his hat over his eyes. When he lifted his hat the young musician had vanished.

The haunting music was often heard near Burgh Hill. Villagers linked it with the accidental death of a youngster at the nearby mansion known as Bramshott Court — itself frequented by a ghostly Quaker. Several of their fraternity were buried in the grounds during the eighteenth century. The apparition, dressed in black with the archetypal Quaker's hat, is said to have been particularly active when Bramshott Court was used as an army hospital during World War I.

Other old Bramshott ghosts include a Royalist soldier and a murdered highwayman, both on horseback; a strange black pig which would suddenly appear — and as quickly disappear — in fields near the church; a phantom pot-boy from the days of coach travel; and a white calf. Two men who followed this bizarre animal ghost one moonlit night claimed that it suddenly shrunk in size until it was no bigger than a cockerel. Then it vanished. The ghosts of a family group, mother and children, also haunt the village and a crowd of phantoms wearing sixteenth-century costume has appeared in Wolmer Lane.

One of those ubiquitous Hampshire coaches frequently rumbles along Rectory Lane and past the church of St Mary the Virgin. Neither coach nor horses are ever seen: the sound ceases if a startled villager peers from a window.

The Church of St Mary the Virgin is haunted by two ghosts.

It was suggested to local historian Roger Newman, who learned of a sighting (or rather a hearing) during the spring of 1971, that the phantom coach carries one of the long-dead Butler family from Downlands Park.

The church itself is also haunted. Although its chancel dates back some seven-hundred years, most of the building is of Victorian origin, and the little girl in a demure poke-bonnet who drifts through the churchyard wall may be the wraith of a child from that period. Another apparition sometimes seen among the gravestones is a run-of-the-mill spectre clad in its white burial shroud.

Bramshott was a staging-post for smugglers during the eighteenth century. One of their tunnels reputedly ran from a secret vault under the church to emerge a short distance up Rectory Lane, away from prying eyes. It passed beneath an Elizabethan building known as Adams Cottage and when there is a smuggler's moon the trundle of brandy barrels may still be heard as the old ruffians ply their trade even after death.

The picturesque cottage derives its name from the Adams family,

A phantom keeper has been seen at his former home, Adams Cottage.

successive generations of whom were employed as forest keepers from as far back as the mid-sixteenth century. One of them reputedly returns to his former home from time to time. The smiling ghost of a tall young man in brown clothing is said to have appeared at least once inside the cottage; more often he has been seen in the garden, sometimes standing but on other occasions sitting with a clay pipe in his mouth.

There have been reports, too, of a female spirit haunting Adams Cottage, her presence betrayed by a strong floral perfume. Presumably it is she who was responsible for surprising the occupants who used to find their blankets neatly turned back at bedtime.

Behind the church is Covers Farm, hundreds of years old and named after the Cover family, prominent local landowners who owned it from the late-seventeenth century. Now it is a farm in name only. Miss Patricia Halahan has lived in the small farmhouse since 1970 without, she tells me, seeing or hearing anything of its ghostly Grey Lady.

The ghost of a drowned woman often appeared at Covers Farm.

It was a different story not too many years ago. Farm workers, visitors and the farmer himself often saw the apparition of a young woman wearing a grey dress or shroud at Covers Farm. She was widely believed to be the earth-bound spirit of a suicide who drowned herself in the farmhouse well. Nearly one-hundred feet deep and now securely covered, the well can still be seen in the kitchen. According to Roger Newman, the tragedy occurred at a time when the local Workhouse authorities rented the building to house paupers who laboured in the nearby stone quarries. He suggests that the unfortunate woman may have been a domestic at the farm, but nobody knows what drove her to kill herself.

The ghost of another woman who drowned herself at Bramshott also finds itself drawn back to the scene of her death. In 1745 or 1746 the body of a local woman, Elizabeth Butler, was discovered in the little river that flows through meadows near Bramshott Vale, and now her unhappy wraith is seen drifting across the fields or walking along the river bank.

Bramshott Manor House looks much the same today as it did during the fifteenth century, although nowadays it is surrounded by more modern homes.

A ghostly soldier on horseback rode from the doors of Crondall Lodge. (See page 29)

Believed to be the oldest continuously inhabited house in Hampshire, the attractive building is said to have two ghosts as permanent residents. One is a white-clad female apparition who may be the shade of a former lady of the manor, Lady Hole.

An Elizabethan rector is reputedly the more persistent revenant. Edmund Mervyn's wealthy father allowed him to use the manor house as the village parsonage and it was there that the priest ended his days after enduring many years' imprisonment in London for his religious beliefs. Mervyn's ghost is said to appear inside the house, usually on the first floor, and in its peaceful garden. Like Keeper Adams, the rector means no harm: both seem content simply to revisit the homes they loved in life.

Bramshott's supernatural population shows no signs of diminishing. As I left Covers Farm in the summer of 1992, a villager who knew of my interest assured me that the ghost of film actor Boris Karloff frequents the local cottage where once he lived. The master of horror could not have returned to a more haunted village. 🦇

CRONDALL

White-faced and trembling with fear, a young man rushed home through the quiet midnight streets of Crondall. His enjoyable night out at a December dance in the neighbouring village had ended with a frightening experience he was to remember for the rest of his life.

It was during the early years of World War II that Alfred Crooks, then about seventeen years of age, saw a ghost. He was alone, having recently parted from a friend with whom he had walked back from Crookham after the dance. His route through Crondall led him along Croft Lane, a stretch of which is bordered on one side by the ancient churchyard of All Saints' Church and on the other by the walls of Crondall Lodge. The peace of the village street was suddenly broken by the sound of knocking. It came from the double doors of Crondall Lodge.

To young Alfred's astonishment, a horse bearing a man in armour then appeared through the doors. Its hooves clattered as it crossed Croft Lane and passed directly through the churchyard wall as though the obstacle did not exist.

The ghostly steed moved away from him, up the straight avenue of lime trees that leads through the churchyard to the church porch. Alfred distinctly heard a number of heavy thuds when horse and rider reached the porch. It sounded as if the soldier was thumping on the church door, the shaken young man told his family when he arrived home. Never again could he be persuaded to pass the area after dark, so frightening was his experience.

Phantom soldiers have been seen at Crondall church for at least a hundred years. Many fighting men lost their lives during military engagements fought in and around the village during the Civil War and it is said that the ghosts are echoes of that seventeenth-century conflict.

The church itself is much older. Norman in origin and with preserved records dating back for more than four-hundred years, the stoutly buttressed building is noted for its splendid early-English rib-vaulted chancel. Equally pleasing is the beautiful avenue of limes bordering a path of brick and flint along which the ghostly armoured man rode.

He is believed to have been one of Cromwell's men, killed during the

All Saints' Church, where phantom soldiers have been seen and heard.

Civil War. The Parliamentarian commander described Crondall as 'a hazardous outpost' while he was battling to take Alton, and hundreds of Cromwell's troops were stationed in the village from 1643 as Sir William Waller prepared to attack the Royalist stronghold of Basing House, some ten miles away. They occupied All Saints' Church, whose sturdy walls provided an ideal fortress, throwing up defensive earthworks and digging entrenchments around its ancient stones. Still the King's men attacked them in a series of bloody skirmishes. Not until October 1645 was the long and bitter siege of Basing House brought to an end.

Small wonder, then, that ghostly Roundheads haunt Crondall. Many villagers reported seeing the apparition of a foot-soldier near the church towards the end of the last century, and a personal account of one such appearance was recorded by Stephen Darby, an enthusiastic ghost hunter of the period.

Darby's other passion was old churches. While visiting his cousin Sarah at Crondall during 1899, he accepted her suggestion to take his sketch book along to All Saints', where some restoration work had just been completed. Darby was engrossed in his drawing when he happened to glance towards the driveway of a house opposite the church gate. From his description it is probable that the house in question was the Old Parsonage, a seventeenth-century building at the junction of Croft Lane with Church Street.

He was intrigued to see a strangely-dressed man walk from the driveway, cross the road and enter the churchyard. Darby assumed from his clothing that he must have been participating in a pageant or village play. He was dressed as a Roundhead trooper, complete with armoured breastplate under a leather jerkin. Black leather thigh-boots and a round helmet with large cheek-flaps completed his costume.

The figure walked through the churchyard and into the church, followed by Stephen Darby. Only later did it occur to him that the soldier's boots had made no sound on the stone floor as he strode down the nave to kneel before the altar. Darby moved behind a pillar, trying to obtain a better view, and in those few moments the figure vanished. During a thorough but fruitless search of the old church he discovered that only the main door was unlocked, and he would have noticed had the soldier left by it.

His growing realisation that the Roundhead was not of this world was confirmed when he met the vicar outside the church and told him what he had seen. There was no village pageant, said the priest, but several parishioners had reported sightings of the phantom soldier over the years.

Another Roundhead ghost — it might have been the same mounted apparition seen by Alfred Crooks — appeared within fifty years of Darby's experience. The only known record of this manifestation comes in a letter published by a local newspaper sometime during the Second World War. Above the signature 'L.A.D.' appeared the following account:

'Last night, Wednesday 2 November, being a very fine moonlit night, a friend suggested that we should enjoy an hour's cycle ride before turning in. So off we went to Crondall. The time was 10.15 pm when we reached the church. We had left our cycles against the wall of the churchyard and we were about to enter the gate to walk up the lime avenue to the church when we were attracted by a misty object coming, it seemed to us, from a carriage drive opposite the wall.

'We stood perfectly still and waited to see what it really was when, to our utter amazement, we saw it was a rider on horseback, dressed in what looked

The haunted avenue of lime trees in the churchyard of All Saints' Church.

like the armour of Cromwellian days. Whatever it was rode right through the churchyard wall, up the avenue and disappeared, it seemed to us, into the church. We waited about half-an-hour, hoping it would return, but we did not see it again'.

According to Dorothea St Hill Bourne, a supernatural incident may have been responsible for disturbing the marriage ceremony at Crondall church of a member of the Lefroy family, which for a hundred-and-fifty years owned Itchell Manor House — itself heavily haunted until its demolition in 1954. Katherine Lefroy's wedding service was interrupted by what seemed to be the heavy tramp of a man's footsteps walking backwards and forwards along the church roof. It sounded like the boots of an armed man, one of the congregation said later.

The ceremony was halted while a male relative of the bride rushed up to the roof to investigate. No one was there, neither had anyone been seen by a group of well-wishers standing in the churchyard. To add to the mystery, the church roof has been altered substantially over the centuries. No man could have clumped along it with such apparent confidence. No mortal man, that is.❦

FARNBOROUGH

The charming manor house known as Broomhill manages to preserve an ageless serenity, despite being hemmed in nowadays by the red-brick homes of a Cove housing estate.

Parts of the building are believed to date from the late-thirteenth century, when William de Bromhulle resided there, and the ancient manorial courts were held in the old house with its three wells and double inglenook fireplaces until 1925. Many notable owners have come and gone over the years, and some sources claim that it was used as a monastery for a while. Now, perhaps ignominiously for such an historic house, it is used as showrooms for the sale of reproduction furniture.

An indication of Broomhill's permanent resident comes in the form of a large mural in an upstairs corridor. Drawn by a friend of the present tenants, it depicts a rather sinister monk, and indeed a phantom brother is reputed to haunt the house. I understand that his presence has long been felt there and that his shadowy form was seen by at least two people on separate occasions not too many years ago.

Sightings of a more modern spectre have been reported in Farnborough itself. The town accommodates the Aerospace Division of the Defence Research Agency, previously known for years as the Royal Aircraft Establishment, to where the remains of a light aircraft were taken in 1964 for examination by air accident investigators. With it, some say, came the ghost of its pilot.

Nancy Spain, one of the foremost tabloid journalists of her day, died when the plane she was piloting crashed as she flew to cover the Grand National for the *Daily Express*. The wreckage was taken to an accident investigation hangar at Farnborough, since when there have been occasional reports of the writer's ghost appearing in the nearby car park.

An imposing white manor house known as Farnborough Place has long had the reputation of being haunted. It has housed St Peter's junior school since 1962 but previously during this century it served successively as a private dwelling, a hotel, a nursing home and the headquarters of Power Jets. Sir Frank Whittle, pioneer of jet propulsion, is just one of many famous names associated

A phantom monk is said to haunt Broomhill in Pennine Way, Cove.

with the building's long history.

The site has been occupied since Anglo-Saxon times. Parts of the present house reputedly date back to the early-thirteenth century, when the manorial lords, the de Farnburgh family, made it their home. Ownership passed to Sir Thomas Cheyne during the fourteenth century and to Edward Dickinson in 1619. For many years a plaque on the nearby church wall commemorated his daughter, the great-grandmother of eccentric novelist and humorist Laurence Sterne.

By 1652 the manor house was occupied as one of their family seats by the Annesleys, the Earls of Anglesey. Nell Gwynne, mistress of Charles II, was their frequent guest at Farnborough Place, an association which may account for the subsequent haunting. Her ghost is said to have been seen there on numerous occasions over the centuries, and some people believe that Nell is responsible for all the strange happenings at the old manor house.

Farnborough Place, where a ghostly figure in a brown robe has appeared.

Its present appearance owes much to a major reconstruction carried out during Queen Anne's reign, reputedly by Sir Christopher Wren. The restored property was bought in 1768 by the Wilmot family, and Sir Joshua Reynolds and David Garrick were among the notables entertained there by 'The Giant', Henry Wilmot. Charles Kingsley also visited from his home at Eversley. The house was subsequently home to several families until with the death of Major Carlyon it became a hotel.

It was during this period, soon after the Second World War, that Albert Bailey accepted an invitation from the hotel proprietor to search for a secret tunnel. Mr Bailey's ancestors had lived in the area for some two-hundred years, so he had often heard rumours that an underground passage linked the cellars of Farnborough Place with the crypt of nearby St Peter's Church.

In an article in *Hampshire* magazine (December 1966) he describes how he joined a group of young men in smashing their way through the cellar wall. After four nights' work — the wall was two feet thick — they were disappointed to find themselves in an adjoining cellar which could have been reached by another door. The hotel caretaker undertook to continue searching for the tunnel entrance, but when Albert Bailey arrived the following day he met a frightened man. The caretaker made it very clear that he would never go into the cellars again. Working down there alone, he said, he had experienced a "creepy" feeling, as if someone or something was watching him.

Scoffing at the story, Mr Bailey went down into the cellar, to the spot where the caretaker had been working. As he neared it he "knew a fear I had never known before" as the air became icy cold and he heard a faint whispering. There followed what he imagined to be the soft sound of a harp coming from the old wall.

The music grew louder before abruptly stopping. Then the perfume of roses filled the air and Albert Bailey heard a woman's voice, "slow, cultured and divinely pretty", reciting a short prose poem. His fear left him, to be replaced by a feeling of well-being. It was, he said, a weird experience.

Mr Bailey and his friends later discovered their underground passage. It led to a huge well. In 1992 Mr Howard Newton, a former headmaster at Farnborough Place, told me that he too had been along the secret tunnel towards the church and found his way barred by the well.

Howard Newton was unaware of the building's reputation when his school, St Peter's, moved there in 1962. He never saw a ghost during his six years at Farnborough Place. "But I felt it," he told me. Shortly after the move he found himself alone one summer's evening in what was formerly an attic bedroom. "I was sorting some things out when I suddenly had a cold, shivery feeling," he recalled. "There was a distinct atmosphere of unease in the room. I just knew someone or something was there with me — something not very pleasant."

The headmaster was sufficiently disturbed by the experience to make some enquiries. He learned that others had felt a 'presence' in the same room many years before. It seems that while Farnborough Place was being used as a nursing home one patient after another asked to be moved rather than stay any longer in that attic bedroom. New arrivals would be unaware of what the previous occupants had reported. Sometimes the room would be left unoccupied for long intervals. But patients still complained about its 'uncomfortable' atmosphere and preferred to be accommodated elsewhere.

Mr Newton was also told that after the building had been purchased for conversion into a school, but before St Peter's actually moved in, a bishop had performed an exorcism there after attending evening service at the church. Presumably this was prompted by the previous experiences, and perhaps particularly by what transpired while Farnborough Place was used as a jet engine college during the 1950s.

Reports of supernatural phenomena were commonplace then. Scientists, naval officers and jet engineers — notoriously pragmatic men — were numbered among those who saw or heard things beyond their comprehension. Events reached such a pitch that the college introduced lectures to reassure students attending courses that the building's ghost was harmless.

One engineer was awakened by the sound of someone walking above his bedroom ceiling. Knowing the room above should have been unoccupied, he ventured out to investigate, only to be thoroughly frightened by hearing disembodied footsteps coming down the stairs towards him. He fled back into bed.

On another occasion a Royal Navy commander who had no idea the place was haunted found himself wide awake in the middle of the night, icy cold with fear, and with his hair "literally standing on end." The college principal, Mr Donald Brown, was not surprised. He himself often heard sounds that he described at the time as "the ghost walking about."

Some people not only heard the ghost. They saw it. The college housekeeper reported several personal sightings of an apparition dressed in a long brown robe and a large hat. It would drift silently into view, she said, vanishing as quickly as it had appeared. Another woman was cycling up the drive one day when she saw what she took to be the housekeeper. But the spectre simply walked into a tree and disappeared as the cyclist approached.

If, as Howard Newton was told, an attempt was made to exorcise the spirit after these events, it does not seem to have been totally successful. Besides his experience in the old attic room, at least two other staff members have detected an unwelcome presence at Farnborough Place.

Office assistant Winnie Sims has worked there since about 1970. Not

Hinton Ampner House, built fifty yards from the site of the haunted manor house. (See page 39)

long after taking up her post she happened to be in the cellars where Albert Bailey and the hotel caretaker had stood some twenty-five years previously. Her experience was remarkably similar to theirs. "I was alone, yet suddenly I had the definite feeling that somebody else was there," she told me. "It felt as if someone was peering over my shoulder. It wasn't at all pleasant."

Disturbing events have occurred as recently as July 1992. According to Mrs Sims a fellow employee has heard inexplicable noises while working alone in the old manor house. Lights which he has turned off switch themselves back on, and he often has an eerie feeling that someone is behind him in the deserted building.❦

HINTON AMPNER

Few of Hampshire's classic ghost stories are as remarkable or as well-documented as the haunting at Hinton Ampner, near Alresford. The strange events in its Tudor manor house during the late-eighteenth century were recorded at the time in letters which still exist, and in a detailed account recorded for her children by Mary Ricketts, a lady with an unimpeachable reputation for truthfulness. Other witnesses to the veracity of the story include her brother, Capt. John Jervis, later created Lord St Vincent for his illustrious naval exploits.

The ghosts of Hinton Ampner are believed to have been those of a former owner, Lord Stawell, his sister-in-law, Honoria Stewkeley, and his bailiff, Isaac Machrel. These three, it was said, had shared the guilty secret that Lord Stawell and Honoria were lovers after — and possibly before — the death of his wife. There were whispers too that an illegitimate child of this liaison had been murdered.

Honoria Stewkeley died in 1754. Apoplexy killed Lord Stawell in his drawing room the following year and shortly afterwards Machrel died under a falling stack of wood. It was not long before Lord Stawell's groom was horrified by the appearance of his dead master's ghost, moving about his former bedroom wearing the 'drab-coloured' clothing which he had favoured in life, and during the following years other sightings of his apparition were reported. None of this was known to William and Mary Ricketts when they took the tenancy of the manor house in January 1765, but they soon realised that they had made an unfortunate choice for their new home.

From the moment they took up residence inexplicable footsteps were heard. Doors would suddenly slam, or slowly open and close of their own accord. Suspecting a prankster, Mr Ricketts had all the locks changed, but the disturbances continued. Mournful groans and rustlings for which no cause could be found began to be heard in various parts of the house.

Then the ghosts appeared. The children's nurse was frightened at seeing a man wearing a drab-coloured suit enter Mrs Ricketts's bedroom, and one night a groom saw a similar apparition elsewhere in the house. On another occasion a woman dressed in a dark silk dress rushed downstairs, along a passage and into the yard, passing an open kitchen door where she was seen clearly by a group of servants; but a man who was coming in from the yard saw nothing, neither was such a woman visiting the house at the time.

Late in 1769 Mr Ricketts left for the West Indies on business. Almost every night thereafter his wife and children were disturbed by heavy footsteps and a rustle like the movement of a stiff silk dress in her bedroom. The solid tramp of a man's tread became commonplace throughout the house, marching along passageways to stop outside rooms or seeming to walk through solid walls. His phantom footsteps once came right to the foot of Mary Ricketts's bed where she lay wide awake and terrified.

Other sounds were heard, heavy thumping noises, loud knocks on doors and strange music. A hollow murmuring often filled the house, swelling in volume like a rising wind, even when the air outside was still.

The situation had become unbearable by the summer of 1771. Unearthly screams and shrieks would suddenly alarm the household. Mrs Ricketts felt 'indescribable terror' on one occasion when a hideous noise erupted very near to her. Ghostly mutterings were heard, night after night, as if two men and a shrill-voiced woman were conversing, although the words were indistinguishable.

A manservant who had lived in the area for many years heard a voice calling him to a window on three occasions; nobody was ever there, but he recognised the harsh, guttural voice of Isaac Machrel. And a nurse who foolishly expressed disappointment that she had heard little of the eerie noises was assailed by a hideous shriek, passed out with shock and then was plagued every night until she left Hinton Ampner.

Mary Ricketts's brother, Captain Jervis, was told about the alarming events when he visited her that summer. Seeking a rational explanation, the pragmatic naval officer arranged to keep armed watch with his manservant and a Captain Luttrell. After thoroughly searching the house and locking all the doors, the three men prepared for their night's vigil.

No sooner was Mary Ricketts in bed than she heard a silk skirt rustle in her room. Luttrell's bedroom door immediately slammed open and an unseen presence moved past him, followed by the sound of footsteps going towards Mrs Ricketts's bedroom. With pistols cocked the three men searched the area without result, but for the rest of that night loud crashes and the slamming of doors shook the building. Baffled by an experience beyond his comprehension,

Several people have felt a strange presence in the magnolia garden at Hinton Ampner House.

the future Lord St Vincent advised his sister to leave at the earliest opportunity.

He and Captain Luttrell kept watch at Hinton Ampner every night for a week while alternative accommodation was sought for Mrs Ricketts and her children. And each night they fruitlessly investigated the source of deep groans, rustlings, whispered conversations, heavy pounding on doors and loud footsteps. Finally the Bishop of Winchester gave Mary Ricketts the use of Wolvesey Palace and she moved out. Her family never returned to the haunted house.

No natural cause of the frightening disturbances was ever found, despite the substantial rewards offered by Mr Ricketts and by Lord Stawell's daughter, Lady Hillsborough. A Mr Lawrence next took the tenancy at Hinton Ampner for a brief period, forbidding his servants to mention anything they might see or hear there. There were unconfirmed reports of the woman's ghost appearing during Lawrence's tenancy, and certainly something seems to have made him suddenly quit the house. The haunted building then remained unoccupied — at least by earthly beings — for twenty years until eventually it was torn down.

A curious discovery was made during its demolition in 1793. In a box concealed under the floor of a lobby near what had been Mrs Ricketts's bedroom was a very small skull, possibly that of a monkey or an infant. No expert examination appears to have been made at the time, but if the skull was human it may serve to confirm those rumours of Lord Stawell's murdered bastard child.

All that remains of that dreadful house are the walled kitchen garden and the stables. Soon after its destruction the then Lord Stawell built another house less than fifty yards away. Substantially altered and extended over the years, it passed to his descendants, the last private owner being Ralph Stawell Dutton, sometime High Sheriff of Hampshire, who became Lord Sherborne. In 1984 it was bequeathed to the National Trust under his will, so today the public can visit the site of one of Hampshire's most notorious haunted houses.

Do the spirits of Machrel, Stawell and his paramour lurk there still? Nick Brooks, administrator of Hinton Ampner House, told me, "No ghosts or disturbances have been reported recently, although I understand that some strange noises for which no explanation could be found used to be heard in the new house. And since the grounds were opened to the public many visitors have experienced a distinct feeling of unease in the magnolia garden, on what used to be the north side of the old manor house."❣

LIPHOOK

Queen Anne had been on the throne just a few years when William Stone rebuilt a coaching inn at Liphook. It was a wise investment. The Blue Anchor occupied a prime position on the London to Portsmouth road, and the main business rival had been eliminated when his predecessor, Mrs Elizabeth Keen, shrewdly bought and closed down the Crown, where Samuel Pepys had stayed in 1668. Furthermore, the Anchor enjoyed an excellent reputation dating back some four-hundred years to the days when Edward II had lodged there while hunting. Other royal patrons had included Elizabeth I, James I and Charles II.

The inn was often visited by Queen Anne herself before landlord Stone died in 1725. Sixty-four years later the Royal Anchor came into being when George III granted the establishment its 'royal' prefix after staying there with Queen Charlotte.

Captain Jack's ghost haunts the room where he was killed.

Their son, the Prince Regent, joined the tally of notable guests. So did John 'Liberty' Wilkes, Nelson and the Duke of Wellington: he lunched there with the Prussian Prince Blucher and other allied leaders after Waterloo. William IV followed, and Victoria with her beloved Albert. The famous Royal Anchor was a flourishing enterprise, where during the heyday of horse transport up to two-dozen coaches a day stopped to change teams.

But it had a less savoury clientele. Once there were chains and heavy iron rings in the cellars and around the fireplaces, where convicts bound for Portsmouth's prison hulks or for transportation to the colonies were shackled overnight. It used to be said that the ghosts of some of those wretches roamed the building at dead of night.

And there were the highwaymen. A gang led by James Fielding, vicar of Lynchmere, frequented the Anchor during the eighteenth century, alert for information about wealthy travellers using the coaching routes, and among their number was the notorious Captain Jack, otherwise known as Jacke or Jacques.

His criminal career ended when the Excise men trapped him in a first-floor room at the Anchor.

Some accounts say that Jack was shot dead while hiding up the chimney, others that he tried to escape into a secret passage through a concealed fireside bolt-hole. A more improbable yarn tells of the highwayman eluding capture by hiding in the chimney, where he became inextricably stuck, and goes on to report that his skeleton was found there ten years later.

The Royal Anchor is a pub and restaurant now, but the small room with its bay window and brick chimney where Captain Jack met his death is still there. So is the highwayman's ghost. An Australian tourist actually saw the phantom, not too many years ago, when the historic building was still a hotel.

She had no idea that room 6, her bedroom at the front of the building, was haunted, neither had she heard the tale of Captain Jack. Probably it would not have worried her: the woman seems to have possessed true Aussie grit. After spending just one night at the Anchor, she came down to breakfast and calmly asked the then landlord whether there was a ghost in the building.

On three separate occasions during the night she had seen the figure of a man emerge from her bedroom fireplace, walk across the room and pass through the door. More intrigued than frightened, the woman followed him the third time it happened, only to see him vanish in the passage at the top of the stairs. She told the landlord that the silent figure was dressed in the long coat and tricorn hat traditionally favoured by English highwaymen.

Captain Jack has his room to himself these days. The present landlord, Gary Treacher-Evans, has used it as a store for his golf clubs since taking over the Royal Anchor in 1989. "People tell me he's up there and I have had telephone calls from as far away as America enquiring about the ghost," he told me. "But I've yet to see him."

An early engraving depicts the Tedworth Drummer as a demon.
(From Joseph Glanvill's 'Saducismus Triumphatus', 1683)

TIDWORTH

Magistrate John Mompesson was away in London when a drum was confiscated from a vagrant discharged soldier and taken to his Tidworth home to await his return. He arrived back to hear alarming news from his frightened wife and servants. Soon after the drum had been lodged with them, loud noises of drumming and thumping were heard, sounds that disturbed their sleep at intervals throughout the night. Witnesses even spoke of seeing the drum rise into the air to be beaten by unseen hands.

So began a classic series of hauntings. They lasted for several years during the early 1660s, spreading the fame of Tidworth throughout the country. The village was known as Tedworth in those days and the episode is still referred to as 'The Drummer of Tedworth'. Some versions say it happened in what is now

South Tidworth, Hampshire, others plump for North Tidworth, which is in Wiltshire; but the county boundary was then so ill-defined that the story may properly find a place in this book.

Witchcraft or demons were blamed at the time for the strange events at John Mompesson's house. They are recognised today as having been typical poltergeist activity. As with similar phenomena, children were involved — Mompesson had two little girls — and it may be significant that things were quiet when the youngsters stayed temporarily at another house.

The hauntings began after the arrest of William Drury, a former regimental drummer who 'went up and down the country to show hocus-pocus, feats of activity, dancing through hoops and such like devices'. Drury was travelling to Portsmouth when he was charged with using forged documents to obtain money. Mompesson released him but retained the drum which the old soldier used during his act. The magistrate was to regret his decision, because within a few days he was nearly demented after almost continuous nightly drumming.

Even after he destroyed the drum there was no respite from the noise. It was on the outside of the house at first but after a month the sound was heard, four or five nights a week, from the room where the drum had lain. It was a beating 'like that at the breaking up of a Guard', according to the Reverend Joseph Glanvill, Fellow of the Royal Society and chaplain to Charles II, who came to investigate the strange stories reaching London.

Glanvill found much to report. Events worsened. Children levitated into the air, uncanny blue lights and sulphurous smells manifested themselves, chairs and household objects flew around, chamber pots were emptied onto beds, and sleepers awoke to feel heavy weights on their stomachs and feet. 'Some have had their hands catched as they have been feeling for a chamber pot,' wrote Glanvill.

A manservant, 'a stout fellow of sober conversation', regularly had his bedclothes pulled off. On other occasions he felt something forcibly restraining his hands and feet, as if he were being tied up, and his shoes were thrown at his head.

Mompesson's children attracted particular attention. Their nightclothes and hair were often pulled by invisible hands. Independent witnesses watched as an unseen agency pulled them from their beds into the air one night, banging their legs against the bedposts until they were black and blue. Glanvill himself was present when a scratching sound was heard from behind their bolster, followed by a noise similar to a dog panting under the bed. It lasted half an hour. He and an associate searched the room thoroughly without finding anything, noting carefully that the two children, who were in bed throughout, could not have made the scratching noises as their hands were always in full view.

A minister named Craig found his leg struck softly by a bedstaff in the children's room on another occasion. And on November 5, 1662, before a room full of witnesses, a wooden board in the same bedroom rose and moved towards a servant, who thrust it back and forth with an invisible being until Mompesson rebuked him for being too 'familiar' with it.

No rational explanation was found for the Tidworth (or Tedworth) hauntings. Even a Royal Commission appointed to investigate by Charles II confessed itself baffled. As for William Drury, he was sentenced to transportation early in 1663 for stealing pigs at Gloucester. Escaping from a convict ship in the Bristol Channel, the old soldier was re-arrested at Uffcott, near Swindon, after again beating a drum to draw attention to his act.

Mompesson had him charged with witchcraft, claiming that he was responsible for the hauntings, but he was acquitted for lack of evidence. Nevertheless, Drury was transported to Virginia for stealing the pigs and there, presumably, he ended his days.❧

The ancient village of Vernham Dean, haunted by the ghost of a penitent priest.

VERNHAM DEAN

The Great Plague of 1665 killed at least 70,000 people in London. Small wonder, then, that many of the capital's citizens tried to flee the pestilence by moving into the sweeter air of the countryside. In so doing, they carried infection and death to rural communities that otherwise might have gone unscathed.

The remote village of Vernham Dean, tucked away in a corner where Hampshire meets Wiltshire and Berkshire, did not escape. History does not record how many of its inhabitants contracted the virus, but when his parishioners began dying the rector realised where his duty lay. He used the power of his cloth to persuade them into leaving their homes and settling on nearby Conholt Hill, where they could not spread the plague by contact with travellers or by visiting other villages. Some versions of the story say they moved into a pest-house or primitive isolation hospital, others that the wretches simply camped as best they could.

At least they were assured of care and provisions. The rector promised to tend the sick, to give decent burial to the dead and to fetch food and other supplies from Andover, charging them in the name of God not to move from their hill. He did not keep his promise.

The charitable version is that he set off with the best of intentions but was himself struck down by the plague. A more cynical view is that the rector deliberately reneged on his vow through fear of visiting the infected encampment. Abandoned by the cleric who had promised faithfully to help them, afraid to leave in case of divine punishment, the villagers of Vernham Dean perished in miserable isolation.

One would expect their spirits to haunt Conholt Hill. Instead, it is the ghost of the rector which has appeared over the centuries. Witnesses who have seen this small and pitiful wraith eternally trudging up the side of the hill have remarked on how it appears stooped and bent almost double, as if carrying some heavy burden. We can but guess whether the weight upon his shoulders is an overwhelming realisation of his cowardice and guilt, or the supplies he promised to provide for his starving flock.

He may have been the phantom man seen in the area by a woman whilst cycling towards her home at Fosbury in 1949. She found herself approaching an indistinct figure dressed in some form of robe which swung as it walked. It was white from the waist upwards, she said, but before she drew close enough to see more detail the shadow simply disappeared among the roadside trees.

WINCHESTER

There were two plays on the bill when I visited the Theatre Royal in Winchester. Was it just by intriguing coincidence that they happened to be *The Way of all Flesh* and *The House of the Spirits*? For indeed spirits have been seen within its walls, as I was to learn from theatre historian Phil Yates.

Brothers John and James Simpkins built the Royal in Jewry Street during 1913 by converting and extending the Market Hotel, which had occupied the site since 1880. After only eight years as a variety house and revue theatre it was used as a cinema from 1922 until its closure in 1974. Strenuous efforts were made to save and refurbish the grand old building, and its doors were reopened to theatre-lovers in 1978. The ghost of John Simpkins surely looks approvingly on the restoration as it drifts around the theatre.

According to Phil Yates, the Simpkins brothers had a slight tiff while they were building the Royal. James arranged for the initials 'JS' to be included on the decorative proscenium arch over the stage, but John thought the engraving should have read 'J & JS'.

James never fulfilled his promise to amend the initials on the cartouche, an omission that aggrieves his brother even after death. His ghost returns periodically to the theatre to see whether James has yet kept his word. John's small office is now a dressing-room, from which his phantom emerges to walk around the back of the circle until it reaches one of the boxes by the stage. From this vantage point the ghost studiously inspects the cartouche before drifting onto and across the stage, through its back wall and into the main dressing-room next to John's former office.

Not too many years ago one of the theatre's stage managers was astonished when she saw an apparition — it may have been ghostly John Simpkins — disappear through the solid back wall of the stage.

Phantom footsteps have been heard climbing the stairs towards the circle, a tread so distinct that it startled the manageress and an assistant of the little pub (now the Theatre Bar) adjoining the Royal. "It happened before the theatre was reopened," Mr Yates told me. "They thought it might be burglars, but when they rushed next door to investigate they found all the doors properly

The ghost of a former owner stalks the Theatre Royal in Jewry Street.

locked and the theatre deserted."

Another mysterious event at the Royal concerned the ghost of a dead soldier. It happened during the First World War. Among the many young men called away to the trenches was one of James Simpkins's spotlight operators, who in those days were known as 'lime-boys'. During a patriotic show called *Soldiers of the King*, an actress on stage looked into the wings and saw the apparition of a British Tommy. She promptly fainted. Simpkins used to assemble his staff for a farewell photograph if one of them joined the armed forces, and when the actress was shown a particular photograph (which, incidentally, has been preserved) she identified the ghostly soldier as the young lime-boy. It transpired that his mother had received a War Office telegram the previous day, notifying the boy's death in action.

Winchester Cathedral and its ancient surroundings have produced many tales of supernatural visitation. Spectral horsemen have been reported here, riding through The Close and down Dome Alley. Walls are no obstacle — the riders pass right through them.

Winchester Cathedral Close, where several phantoms have been seen over the years.

Quite a stir was caused in 1957 with the publication of a photograph taken inside the cathedral by a visitor. It seems to show thirteen ghostly men in medieval clothing standing before the High Altar. No logical explanation has been found by experts who have studied this celebrated picture and another, taken moments before, showing the area to be deserted. Theories that they might be reflections of nearby stone sculptures have been discounted.

The wife of a former cathedral canon became quite accustomed to seeing a ghostly monk in The Close. It always appeared in the garden of number 11, moving across the lawn, before passing through a high garden wall and into the cathedral. An unusual feature of this shadowy figure, she said, was its pronounced limp. When the garden wall was demolished some time later, three skeletons were unearthed nearby. Experts pronounced the bones old enough to have been the remains of members of a medieval order of monks and, intriguingly, one of the skeletons bore evidence of an arthritic knee — which could well have caused a limp.

A crinolined lady has appeared frequently in a nearby house, 7 Dome Alley, which for some twenty-five years was home to Mrs Janet Crocker, daughter of Sir Samuel and Lady Gurney-Dixon. She often heard footsteps outside the house when no one was there, and what she described as "the regular drumming of feet, as if on stone paving."

Ghostly footsteps were also heard inside the house, in whose drawing room several people have reported seeing the apparitions of children gathered about a spectral woman reading to them from a book. Mrs Crocker called this family group "the happy ghosts". And the old nursery was haunted by an unseen spirit that knocked softly on the door before slowly opening and closing it. A door on the opposite side of the room would then open and close, as if someone had passed through, and the invisible ghost would return by the same route after about half an hour.

Two of Winchester's historic pubs contain well-documented ghosts. The Hyde Tavern in Hyde Street, reputedly the city's oldest inn, has its origins in the days of Alfred the Great. Henry I built the monastery of Hyde Abbey nearby, and no doubt many weary pilgrims and travellers found the inn a convenient source of refreshment and lodging.

There is a legend that hundreds of years ago the landlord turned away a poor woman on a winter's night; whether the inn was full or she had insufficient money we do not know, but according to the story the woman's body was found next morning. She had died from cold and hunger.

Her ghost may still haunt the Hyde Tavern, where residents and guests have found their sleep disturbed by a phantom intruder who pulled away their blankets. A former licensee and his wife were among those who suffered. They often awoke in the small hours of the morning to find something unseen slowly dragging the bedclothes from their bed. The licensee's wife was once so annoyed at finding their blanket being pulled that she sat up and threw it into the middle of the room, ordering the invisible spirit to take it and leave her alone.

On other occasions the couple would discover all the blankets in an untidy heap at their bedside when they woke in the morning. A friend of theirs told ghost hunter Jack Hallam about the night she spent in a little spare bedroom. "Sure enough," she said, "I woke at about four in the morning, feeling terribly cold and with my top blanket on the floor." The strange events at the Hyde

Blankets were pulled from beds by the ghost of the Hyde Tavern.

Tavern continued even when special care was taken to make sure that the blankets were securely tucked in.

Another ghostly woman who suffered a tragic end has been seen by staff, visitors and guests at the Eclipse Inn, a quaint, timbered building that from the sixteenth century was the rectory of St Lawrence's church. A wall plaque on the opposite side of the old market square marks this as 'the place of execution of Lady Lisle, 1685, in the roadway', and it is she who haunts the Eclipse.

Lady Alicia Lisle, known to many as Dame Alice, had been widowed for twenty-one years when they chopped off her head. She had lost her husband, a staunch supporter of Oliver Cromwell, to a Royalist assassin in Switzerland, whence he had fled after the Restoration.

After living peacefully for many years at Moyles Court, her ancestral home at Ellingham near Ringwood, Lady Alicia became caught up in the bitter aftermath of the 1685 Monmouth Rebellion when she granted refuge to John Hickes, a well-known Dissenter, and lawyer Richard Nelthorp. At her trial she

Lady Lisle haunts the Eclipse Inn, where she spent her last days.

claimed to be unaware that they had fought for Monmouth at Sedgemoor. Betrayed by a villager, Lady Alicia and the rebels were arrested in the house by a former Cavalier who bore a long-standing grudge against her husband.

The infamous Judge Jeffreys presided over Lady Alicia's trial at Winchester for harbouring the 'traitor' Hickes. In one of the most shameful episodes of the notorious Bloody Assize, Jeffreys bullied witnesses in his determination to secure the old lady's conviction, finally over-ruling the sympathetic Hampshire jurymen who found in her favour. He sentenced Lady Alicia to be burned at the stake, but public outcry and a petition to the king brought some degree of clemency: the sentence was commuted to beheading.

Lady Alicia Lisle spent her last days in a small room on the top floor of what is now the Eclipse. On September 2, 1685, she stepped out from the room below onto a newly-erected wooden scaffold to meet the axeman. "She was old and dozy and died without much concern," reported the official clerk. But her troubled spirit returns from time to time, haunting her little room and the passageways on the upper floors of the pub. (It also frequents Moyles Court — *see* Ringwood).

Author Marc Alexander has documented several supernatural happenings at the Eclipse. A doctor's wife who spent a night in the haunted room, unaware of its reputation, was terrified by the appearance at the foot of her bed of "the grey figure of an old lady". The guest called in vain for help before pleading with the apparition to go away, whereupon it slowly vanished.

A naval officer had a similar experience in that room. He was so frightened when he awoke to find a pale figure standing there that he immediately packed and fled into the night. Not until daylight could he pluck up sufficient courage to return and tell the tale.

Several members of staff, and guests who were deliberately not told about the hauntings, have seen a shadowy grey figure in the passageways or have felt an uncanny presence in the haunted room, sometimes accompanied by a distinct chill. One level-headed young man, an Outward Bound instructor, heard about the ghost only after he had commented at breakfast on the strange feeling that someone had been in his room all night. Women using the first-floor toilet have repeatedly reported "something strange" about the corridor outside, and a cleaner who felt a light touch on her shoulder turned to glimpse a grey form which quickly vanished.

Another woman experienced a feeling of being watched while cleaning the carpet on the first-floor landing at ten o'clock in the morning. She looked over her shoulder and was shaken to see "a tall woman in a long grey woollen dress" standing motionless in a corner. The grey apparition appeared in the same place on a separate occasion, after the maid felt something gently push her.

While it seems reasonable to assume that the phantom of the Eclipse is the shade of Lady Lisle, no explanation is offered for two strange events at Winchester Library in Jewry Street. Erected as the city's corn exchange in 1838, from the early 1900s the building was in turn a roller-skating rink, a theatre and a cinema before being converted into a library in 1936.

Philippa Stevens, the County Local Studies Librarian, has worked there since 1967. She assured me that she finds nothing unpleasant about the old building's atmosphere, a sentiment not shared by those members of staff who find it 'scary' and prefer not to stay after dark.

Mrs Stevens told me of a morning, early in 1992, when the caretaker was alone in the library at seven o'clock. A pragmatic man, ex-Royal Navy and Prison Service, he was more surprised than startled to hear "very positive footsteps", as if someone was walking along the gallery that runs around the

Phantom footsteps and singing have been heard in Winchester Library, a former corn exchange.

main room. But nobody was there, and although he searched from top to bottom the caretaker found no sign of an intruder in the locked building.

The vaulted, stone-floored basement or cellar of the former corn exchange still lies beneath the library. Not long after she began working there, Mrs Stevens was alone in the quiet basement store when she heard a man singing an operatic aria. "There was no music, just a very faint but distinct voice," she told me. "I was beneath the main library entrance, and I moved along the basement to look out through an old delivery hatch, just in case the sound was coming from the street. No one was there. I could still hear the faint singing when I returned to my original position."

Mystified, she went upstairs to fetch another woman, but when they returned the ghostly singer had obviously departed. The library is completely detached from other buildings and no natural explanation has been forthcoming for Philippa Stevens' puzzling experience. As she says, "You don't expect to hear grand opera sung in a library basement!"

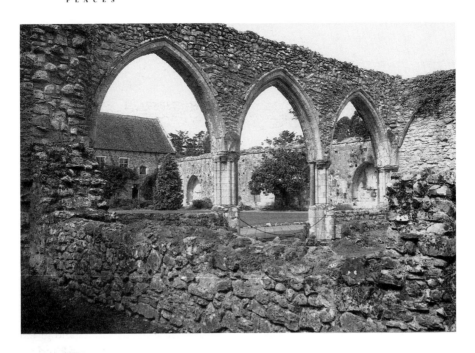

THE SOUTH-WEST

BEAULIEU

The magnificent abbey at Beaulieu reputedly owed its very existence to a supernatural event. It seems that in 1201 a group of Cistercian monks from Berkshire had the temerity to petition ruthless King John for exemption from taxation, whereupon the enraged tyrant ordered their immediate imprisonment. The following day, he decreed, their abbots would be trampled to death by his horsemen.

That night the despot had a vivid dream in which he was tried for his cruelty and condemned to be flogged by the monks. Tradition has it that he found livid whip marks on his body when he awoke. This occult warning, coupled with advice from his chaplain, prompted the king to release his prisoners and grant the Cistercian Order ten-thousand acres of the New Forest on which to build an abbey church with dwellings, a port and a farm. The Cistercians worked and worshipped at Beaulieu for more than three-hundred years until their peace was shattered when Henry VIII dissolved the monasteries.

The brothers have gone, most of their beautiful abbey destroyed, but their spirits return to the place where in life they found tranquillity and security. Phantom monks, ethereal chanting, the smell of incense, unexplained footfalls — all and more have been experienced at Beaulieu, where the supernatural is almost commonplace.

Many villagers accept the presence of revenant monks as naturally as they do one another. Newcomers, however, have been known to pack and leave their estate houses upon learning that the apparently substantial figures encountered working in the fields or walking through the lanes are not of this world.

Top left: The ruins of Beaulieu Abbey, haunted by the phantoms of long-dead monks.

Left: Beaulieu's haunted Domus Conversorum was originally the lay brothers' refectory.

As recently as 1979, a visitor returning from a walk through the vineyard near the abbey ruins expressed surprise that monks still worked there, as he had seen one tending the vines. But there are no monks on the estate or anywhere in the neighbourhood.

Most of the ghosts seen at Beaulieu over the years have been those of the 'brown monks'. The colour of their habits distinguished these labouring lay brothers from the 'white monks', who had taken Holy Orders. A spectral brown monk was often seen during the 1920s in the lanes around the village, in the abbey cloisters and near a medieval winepress. He seemed to be drawn particularly to the Domus Conversorum, the lay brothers' refectory, which now houses an exhibition about monastic life.

Among the many people who saw this friendly wraith was a lady who at that time occupied a flat above the Domus. According to the Hon. Mrs Elizabeth Varley, Lord Montagu's elder sister, Miss Aimee Cheshire claimed to be psychically gifted. She regularly communicated with the spirit monks, knew them by name and made extensive notes about what they told her. Mrs Varley's father later showed the notes to an abbot from Dijon in France, who was astonished by their accuracy and the previously unknown details they revealed about life in an early-English monastery.

Footsteps of long-dead monks and the clanking of their heavy keys have been heard in and around the Domus. Sometimes their singing would fill the air, ceasing as abruptly as it had begun. Miss Cheshire took particular delight in recalling an occasion when friends being entertained to dinner in her flat openly expressed their doubts about the existence of ghosts. Their scepticism was cured by the sudden but short-lived sound of singing which surrounded the stunned diners, as if an invisible choir was in the room.

In 1941 the Special Operations Executive occupied ten houses on the Beaulieu Manor Estate. The tough agents who trained there before embarking on the most dangerous wartime missions were probably not given to wild imaginings, yet even those brave men and women were shaken by the appearance of ghostly brown monks.

They were seen also by two officers from an anti-aircraft battery based at nearby Buckler's Hard as they drove past the abbey ruins one afternoon. When they returned to their battery the soldiers casually asked their chaplain to which

A ghostly monk sat reading in a recess by the old magnolia tree (right).

monastic order the monks of Beaulieu belonged, as they had seen a group in the abbey grounds. The surprised priest responded truthfully that there were no longer any monks there, and it was established later that none had been visiting Beaulieu.

Another soldier, a retired colonel who lived on the estate, saw a figure dressed all in brown moving towards him down the lane near his home one evening. He noticed particularly its swishing robe, a long garment that reached the ground. A dip in the lane momentarily hid the figure from the colonel's view. Then it vanished.

From the top of a stone stairway outside the Domus in 1965, a retired nurse distinctly saw a brown-habited monk sitting in a recess beside a magnolia tree, apparently reading a scroll. When the woman looked out again a few moments later he was nowhere to be seen, neither could she discover any rational explanation for this clear sighting.

He may have been the same scholastic monk seen by Margaret Rutherford, who besides being a splendid actress was intensely interested in the supernatural. She was strolling around the quiet abbey ruins while filming at Beaulieu for a television documentary entitled *The Stately Ghosts of England* when she encountered a monk sitting reading in the cloisters. He vanished into thin air during the brief moment Miss Rutherford looked away.

One of the few recorded sightings of 'white monks' was reported by three boys in 1957. Forced to abandon a night's fishing by rough weather, they sheltered in an old boathouse from where, in the middle of the night, they spotted a rowing boat heading for the shore. Five figures clad in hooded white robes left the boat and moved off towards the abbey. Came the dawn and the boys could find no evidence of either boat or people having been on the muddy foreshore.

Quite the most remarkable phenomenon at haunted Beaulieu is the beautiful sound of monks chanting, as if the departed brothers were still at their devotions. Several witnesses have experienced it over the years. Always, it seems, the chanting is associated with a death in the locality.

Lord Montagu's sister, Mrs Elizabeth Varley, first heard the ghostly voices from her bedroom window in Palace House one night during her late-teenage years. Engrossed in thought, Miss Montagu suddenly felt "frissons of cold" up and down her back. Only then was she fully aware that the sound of repetitive chanting had been drifting on the night air for quite a while. She memorised the notes sufficiently to sing them the following morning to a family guest, who identified them as a Gregorian chant.

Intrigued, the young woman decided to visit Aimee Cheshire and seek her opinion. Before explaining why she had come, she played the notes of the chant on Miss Cheshire's piano. She was astonished when the other at once recognised the tune, saying that she too had heard the chanting the previous night. Miss Montagu was to hear it again on several occasions some years later, after she had left Palace House to live in a nearby cottage.

Another person entranced by the haunting sound was the then curator of Beaulieu's motor museum in 1959. It was just before Christmas. Mr Michael Sedgwick had flung open his cottage window to clear the room of tobacco smoke after working late into the night when the unmistakable sound of chanting was borne on the still air. It was like a Catholic mass, he said, a beautiful chant that swelled and faded in uneven waves as if being broadcast from a faulty radio. In fact, the curator wondered at first if it might be coming from a neighbour's radio and he unsuccessfully tried to find any radio station carrying such a programme.

He heard similar chanting late at night on another occasion, again rising and falling in intensity. And both times he discovered that there had been a death in the village.

Beaulieu's catering manageress, Mrs Bertha Day, heard the ethereal chanting as she returned home late one night. The sound was so clear and convincing that next day she asked the vicar if he had been holding a requiem for a local lady who had died recently. It was beautiful, she said, an experience always to be remembered.

Mr Sedgwick also heard the sounds of a ghostly burial. It happened one night in 1960. From their cottage overlooking a piece of ground that is reputed to have been a graveyard, he and his mother distinctly heard slow, plodding footsteps, indicative of men carrying something heavy. There followed the sounds of digging, a thump and the shovelling of earth. Nothing was seen when the puzzled couple looked from their window at the old burial ground.

The Reverend Robert Powles was entirely convinced of the monks' presence. He was the last of Beaulieu's independent parish priests, owing no allegiance to the bishop, and before his death in 1940 he had served as curate and vicar for some sixty years. He claimed to see and speak regularly with the ghosts and even conducted a special Midnight Mass for them each Christmas Eve behind the locked doors of his church. The monks formed his unseen congregation, he said. Mrs Varley knew him well and had no cause to disbelieve his sincerity. "He always appeared perfectly sane," she recalled in 1980.

'Daddy' Powles, as he was affectionately known to the Montagu family, certainly appears to have been at one with the spirit world. He sometimes spoke of a stormy night when he set out for the home of a dying parishioner who lived on the opposite side of the Beaulieu River.

Arriving in the darkness at what had become a raging torrent, he hurried to cross the bridge but his way was barred by two large, phantom dogs. The priest approached more cautiously. He found the bridge had been swept away and realised that the ghostly animals had prevented him from falling into the turbulent river.

In the New Year of 1916 the Rev. Powles brought strange but comforting news to the Montagu family. They had been notified that John Montagu, the second Baron, was presumed drowned after the P & O liner *Persia* was torpedoed off Crete with the loss of some three-hundred lives. Even *The Times* printed his obituary. But his family should not worry, said Mr Powles, because he knew the baron to be alive: he had seen him walking in front of him in the village. "If he were dead he would have been walking behind me," added the priest. And indeed word was later received that Lord Montagu had been saved.

Mystery also surrounds a discovery that was reported by the national press in 1928. It appears that a local woman encountered a phantom monk, an old man with a grey beard, while walking near the abbey ruins one night. Alternative versions are that she met the ghost in her house, or dreamed of meeting it, or had a vision.

She was commanded to dig at a specified spot among the ruins. There she would find human remains and two round stones. No reason was given for this demand, according to some accounts, but others say that the troubled ghost confessed to having concealed the body of his murder victim, whose remains he wished to be reinterred in sacred ground. Digging unearthed an ancient coffin containing two stones and the bones of a man with a hole in his skull. They were given a Christian burial in accordance with the phantom's request.

The abbey's great gatehouse is now Palace House, Lord Montagu's home. Here, too, there are ghosts. Lord Montagu himself is one of many people who have smelled incense in the upper drawing room, which was formerly a chapel. And for many years there were reports of an evil presence lurking at the top of the stairs, where a butler killed a maid during the nineteenth century.

Something equally dreadful haunts a small room above the 'secret staircase'. A Royalist soldier was slain by Roundhead troops at the top of that staircase during the Civil War. According to Mrs Varley, many people have experienced a feeling of foreboding upon entering the room, and one lady who tried to sleep there was frightened into leaving it in the early hours of the morning by 'something awful' which she refused to discuss.

Alarming, too, were the experiences of a film crew during the making of the documentary *Wonderful Beaulieu*. They had worked late into the night in the upper drawing room when an electrician had occasion to go downstairs alone. He soon returned, badly shaken, to enquire anxiously whether there was

Palace House, Lord Montagu's home, is haunted by several ghosts.

a night watchman in the locked building. There was not. The distressed electrician could never be persuaded to reveal what had frightened him.

Later that night another member of the team heard footsteps following him as he went down the stairs. He assumed it was a colleague, but when the phantom footsteps actually overtook him, moving downstairs, the man fled back to the drawing room, arriving white-faced, cold, and shaking with fear.

An equally terrifying experience befell a cameraman next day as he lined up a shot from the top of a high wall in the abbey ruins. Suddenly an unseen hand took hold of him, pushing him off balance. Other unit members watched in horror as the frightened cameraman pitched forwards, only saving himself from falling by grabbing hold of the stonework.

Anger at being cheated of an inheritance binds the ghost of the second Duke's wife to Palace House. Isabella, Countess of Beaulieu, is believed to be the mysterious Lady in Blue who drifts through the old building. Her apparition has been reported on several occasions over the years.

The old gatehouse where ghostly footsteps climb the stairs each night.

Some of the estate staff who live in harmony with the ghosts recounted their experiences to the *Southern Evening Echo* in 1980. A woman living in the converted stable block was awakened on several occasions by the sound of shuffling feet in a bedroom, where a phantom man has appeared at the foot of her bed. None of this frightened her. "I even find myself talking to the ghosts sometimes," she said at the time. Another employee told how something invisible treads on the stairs leading to a flat in the old gatehouse at precisely ten minutes past ten each night, making them creak.

Even Lord Montagu's butler, Mr Trevor Barnfield, had a story to tell. He responded to a thunderous knocking on his door one night. "No one was there when I opened the door," he said, "but there was no way anyone could have been playing a trick on me."

Sometimes, though, employees find the hauntings too much to bear. Lord Montagu has revealed that in 1964 a staff member and his wife fled from their apartment in the middle of the night and could not be persuaded to return. "Some unearthly body was walking round and round their bed," he said.

I asked Lord Montagu whether he was aware of any recent reports of hauntings. "I am afraid that I have nothing new to add," he replied. That was in May 1992. But on past evidence it would be presumptuous to conclude that the ghosts of Beaulieu have departed. They are still there.☙

BREAMORE

On the edge of the New Forest, just north of Fordingbridge, lies the ancient and picturesque village of Breamore. Pronounce it 'Bremmer' if you wish to please the locals. Besides a flint-walled church built nearly a thousand years ago, its treasures include a mysterious Mizmaze and a beautiful Elizabethan manor house — both of which are haunted.

No one knows who cut the intricate Mizmaze, thirty yards wide, into the downland turf. Some authorities say it dates from prehistoric times, but it is more likely to be of medieval origin. Augustine monks from the long-demolished priory that once stood on the hill knew the maze well, for here they did penance for their misdeeds. Shuffling painfully on bare knees over the hard chalk, misdemeanant monks had to find their way to the centre of the maze and back again. The monks are long gone, but echoes of their cruel punishment linger. Stand near the Mizmaze in the half-light of dusk or dawn and you may hear painful groans and sighs and soft, shuffling noises as the ghostly penitents relive their ordeal.

Breamore House is the home of Mr Edward Hulse, as it has been to nine generations of his family. His ancestor, Sir Edward Hulse, bought the house from Lord Brooke in 1748, acquiring a ghost and an accursed painting into the bargain. An express stipulation of the sale was that a certain picture must remain hanging at Breamore House for ever. According to legend, death within a day comes to whoever even touches the 390-year-old portrait of William Dodington's wife, Christian.

Dodington personally supervised the building of Breamore House, completed in 1583. The Dodington family occupied it until 1660, when it passed with his only surviving grandchild, Anne, upon her marriage to Robert Greville, Lord Brooke. His descendant later sold Breamore to Sir Edward.

Breamore House, where the ghost's appearance presages the owner's death.
(Photo: courtesy Edward Hulse)

As Mr Hulse told me, the Dodingtons were an ill-fated family. Suicide and matricide blighted their lives. On April 11, 1600, sick with worry over a lawsuit pending in the Star Chamber, William Dodington 'went up to St Sepulchre's Steeple, threw himself over the battlements and brake his neck'. It is a 1604 portrait of Mrs Dodington, dressed in mourning clothes after her husband's suicide, which carries the curse.

James I knighted their son William in 1603, but twenty-six years later the family suffered further tragedy when William's wife was murdered in Breamore House by their own son. Henry Dodington paid the penalty at the end of a hangman's noose at Winchester gaol in 1630.

Lady Dodington's ghost haunts the Blue Bedroom where her murder is said to have occurred. Breamore is open to the public and over the years staff and visitors have felt a 'presence' in the room, sometimes accompanied by that

In the portrait, the inscription reads:

ANÕ ÆTAT : 64   DÕNI 1604

CHRISTIAN SISTER TO SIR FRANCIS WALLSINGHAM AND WIFE TO Mʳ WILLIAM DODINGTON WHO BVILT BREAMORE AND MOTHER to Sʳ WILLIAM DODINGTON :

Breamore's accursed portrait of Mrs William Dodington.
(Photo: courtesy Edward Hulse)

inexplicable, marked drop in temperature customarily associated with a haunting. The phantom lady herself, dressed in period costume, rarely appears — much to the relief of the Hulse family. Edward Hulse told me, "It is said if you see the ghost the owner of Breamore House will die. Several people have felt it recently but fortunately none have seen it!"

The portrait of Lady Dodington's mother-in-law still hangs in the Great Hall in accordance with Lord Brooke's condition of sale. Clearly, the Hulse family respect the legend that whoever touches it will die that day. Edward Hulse again: "Our staff are expressly told not to touch the portrait. To do so would be tempting providence and I would feel guilty if anything happened. Certainly I think it would be very unlucky to move it."

Only two people are known to have flouted this advice since World War II. One man decided to put the legend to the test. Depressed over an illness, he deliberately touched the old portrait in a bizarre suicide attempt. He survived. But Mr Hulse also told me about the new handyman who either ignored or overlooked the warning about thirty years ago. He dusted the picture. Later the same day, while erecting a television aerial at his home, he fell from the roof and was killed.

CHILWORTH

Roger and Joan Hamilton knew their search for a new home was over when they found a centuries-old cottage just to the north of Southampton. Walnut Cottage was conveniently close to the city, yet its location in Chilworth Old Village promised the benefits of peace and quiet among pleasant neighbours.

The Hamilton family were told that the timber-framed building, like several others in the village, dated from the seventeenth century. They learned also that originally it comprised two tiny homes, built to house workers from the nearby estate. What they did not realise, and what nobody chose to tell them, was that they were buying a haunted cottage.

Roger Hamilton once scoffed at talk of ghosts. "I was a complete

Picturesque Walnut Cottage has been haunted for more than one-hundred years.

disbeliever before we came to live here," he admitted as we sat in their comfortable lounge. "But what I have seen and heard in this house over the past few years has certainly changed my mind."

He and his wife had an early introduction to their newly-acquired phantoms. The Hamiltons (at their request I am not using their correct names here) decided upon a complete refurbishment before occupying Walnut Cottage in 1987. Being practical people they undertook much of the work themselves, and as the couple entered the bare and empty building one winter evening they were astonished to see a strange light shining from the wooden surface of a downstairs door.

"It was a glowing light, orange-red in colour and about the size of a football," Joan Hamilton recalled. "It slowly faded away as we watched. We could find no explanation. Certainly it was not caused by the setting sun or by a car's headlights — we made sure of that."

On a subsequent evening, as they walked into what is now their lounge to continue work, the unmistakable sound of footsteps came from the room above. A thorough search confirmed that no one else was in the old building.

Only after these two uncanny experiences did they learn through the village grapevine that Walnut Cottage has a remarkable history of hauntings stretching back at least into the early part of the last century. Much of what we know comes from the testimony of the late Mrs Grace MacRae, who occupied the house before the Hamiltons and in whose family it had been since the 1850s. Before then, according to her grandfather, nobody would live there for some years because of repeated ghostly occurrences which on one occasion had driven the frightened occupants into the night.

The hauntings continued after Mrs MacRae's forebears moved in. As her grandparents lay in bed one night they heard footsteps ascending the stairs, followed by the sound of someone washing their hands in the wash basin. They hastily lit a candle, but no one was there and the basin was dry. The same inexplicable sounds, probably unique in the annals of aural hauntings, were heard by Mrs MacRae's husband Donald during the 1940s and by Mrs MacRae herself towards the end of the 1970s.

Phantom footsteps were often heard going up and down the stairs. One of Grace MacRae's childhood memories was of her father and brother getting up many times and searching the house, thinking someone had broken in. When her mother was a child, sharing a bedroom with three sisters, they all heard what sounded like a large animal "bumping up the stairs" and into their room.

Her parents became accustomed to hearing loud crashes and sounds like the smashing of china, noises that she and her husband also heard on numerous occasions after they moved in following their marriage in 1939. Donald MacRae slept alone in the cottage for a month or two before the marriage. One night he heard people talking in low voices and seemed to see old men sitting chatting round the fire, wearing cloth caps with a tassel on one side. "A few weeks later a friend brought a medium to visit us," says Grace MacRae's account. "Although we had not told her of my husband's vision she described the old men and their dress, just as he had seen them."

Other strange events puzzled the newly-weds during their first few years in the isolated cottage. Mrs MacRae again: "We had a very strong letter box and time and time again it would sound as though a letter was being pushed through. There was nothing there. The spring of the letter box was so strong it would be impossible for the wind to move it.

"At that time I would be doing housework and something would fall down behind me with a swish and a sound as of a metal bar falling. This happened at least a dozen times. My husband and I once heard a very loud rat-a-tat on the door. The dog barked but there was no sign of anyone."

One day during the early 1950s Grace MacRae and her mother were surprised to hear the clatter of hooves at the back door, as if a number of horses had trotted up. Nothing was there when they looked out. And on a hot summer night in 1971, while sleeping downstairs, Mrs MacRae heard a crowd of people walk up the path to the front of the cottage, talking in low voices, but again no one was to be seen.

Whispering voices were heard also on the upstairs landing on numerous occasions, particularly in the early hours of the morning. Neither Mrs MacRae nor her relations and visitors who reported hearing these muttered conversations could ever discern the actual words.

Sometimes, in the dead of night, the MacRaes would be disturbed by the sound of furniture being moved about downstairs, but upon investigation everything was in order and no explanation could be found for the noises.

The present occupants are not the first to have seen a strange light at the cottage. There may be a link between the glowing door seen by the Hamiltons in 1987 and two earlier fiery phenomena. In 1924 Mrs MacRae's aunt, the late Miss Hilda Smith, was alarmed to find an eiderdown glowing as if it was on fire, but as she tried to beat out the flames with her hands she realised they were perfectly cool. The 'fire' simply disappeared, leaving the eiderdown undamaged.

And one dark November night in 1939 Mr and Mrs MacRae were returning home and about one-hundred yards from the thatched cottage when, in her words, "we saw a great glow spread over the roof around the chimney stack. We thought the cottage was on fire but looked everywhere and found nothing." The mysterious glow had disappeared when they went outside again.

Walnut Cottage is still haunted. The Hamiltons, a thoroughly level-headed couple, have been driven to that conclusion after their experiences

Previous occupants saw "a great glow" spread around the chimney stack.

during the few years they have lived there. Not long after moving in they were in the lounge when they heard thumping and banging from what used to be the kitchen and is now their dining-room. The noises, loud enough to be heard above the television, sounded exactly like furniture being moved about on a bare floor. "We both got up to investigate, but as we walked towards the dining-room the noise stopped," Mrs Hamilton told me. Nothing was out of place in the room — which is carpeted.

Also from that former kitchen they have heard the clink of china, although nowadays there is nothing in the room to make such sounds. And its door, which was the outer door before an extension was built, suddenly blows open for no apparent reason. "It happens so often we make a joke of it now," said Roger Hamilton. "I find myself calling out something like, 'Come on in if you're coming'."

His wife had an uncanny experience while working on hands and knees, sanding down the wooden floorboards of the upstairs landing. "All afternoon I felt a very strong presence behind me, as though someone was there," she recalled, "and I was convinced that I heard a sharp intake of breath." She mentioned this to one of Mrs MacRae's relatives, who said that others had often had the same experience on the landing over the years.

The family have heard "quite a few odd knocks" for which they can find no explanation in various parts of the cottage. And on one occasion Mr and Mrs Hamilton and their son all went to the front door after clearly hearing someone knock, only to find that no one was there.

But the most persistent and inexplicable phenomenon is the phantom footsteps, first heard by the Hamiltons before they moved in. "We have since heard them on numerous occasions while we are in the lounge," Joan Hamilton told me. "Someone walks diagonally across the bedroom above our heads, on bare boards, although the room is carpeted. It is a very common occurrence."

She paused. "I could go on — so many things happen. In the end, you just have to believe it. But we're not in the least frightened. There's nothing unpleasant here and it doesn't upset us."

EAST WELLOW

Young Florence Nightingale's association with East Wellow began when her wealthy family moved into nearby Embley Park, a fine mansion at the end of a three-mile drive through its own parkland. At the conclusion of a remarkable and long life — she was ninety when she died — the heroine of Scutari might have been buried at Westminster Abbey, so great was her fame and her nation's gratitude.

Instead, in accordance with her wishes, Florence shares the family tomb in the peaceful churchyard of St Margaret of Antioch at East Wellow. One face of the Nightingale family memorial bears only the simple inscription 'F.N. — Born 12 May 1820, Died 13 August 1910'.

'The lady with the lamp' worshipped at St Margaret's for many years. With her passing, it seems fitting that her spirit should wish to bind itself to this

The family tomb at East Wellow church where Florence Nightingale lies.

beautiful corner of her beloved Hampshire. There have been several reports over the years of her ghost sitting quietly among the congregation or drifting about the churchyard, and in May 1992 I learned at third-hand of quite a recent appearance. Unfortunately, I have been unable to trace this report to its source.

Perhaps inevitably, some local folk insist on linking Florence Nightingale's ghost with the spectral coach of Embley Park, her former home, but the lady's historical association with the house seems to be the sole foundation for their belief that it carries her wraith.

Sightings of phantom carriages thundering through the Hampshire countryside are legion. The four horses drawing the East Wellow coach gallop from Embley Park, which is now a school, down its drive and along the lanes to St Margaret's church. Sometimes it is claimed that the coach-and-four can only be seen at midnight on New Year's Eve. They used to clatter over a bridge known as the Sounding Arch, but presumably hooves and wheels are heard there no longer since its demolition in 1966. A phantom coachman urges the horses on, according to some reports. Others claim the coach to be driverless.

St Margaret's is a fascinating little church in its own right. Established during the twelfth century, it boasts a wooden bell-tower with a bell dating from 1420 — one of the oldest in the country. Fragments of medieval religious murals can be seen here, as can several mementoes of Florence Nightingale.

Colonel William Morton worshipped at St Margaret's during the seventeenth century. Perhaps he still does. Morton was a republican, one of the regicides who sealed the fate of Charles I, and it is said that his ghost walks between the church and the nearby manor house, which was once his home.

The author Graham J. McEwan describes a puzzling personal experience at St Margaret's in his book *Haunted Churches of England*. It happened during a visit to the church in July 1988. He was sitting beneath the belfry, concentrating on setting up his camera to take photographs, while his wife and a friend were standing near the pulpit. Engrossed with his work, Mr McEwan was only partly aware that the sound of singing was suddenly in the air. It was not very loud, he says, though sufficiently distinct for him to form the impression that it was plainsong. The singing faded away after perhaps twenty seconds.

Mr McEwan joined his wife after taking a few photographs. She too had heard the singing, which she had assumed must have come from some practising choir. But, according to the author, the brief sound could not have drifted from far away as there was no wind that evening. The McEwans were left wondering whether they had "experienced some sort of psychic phenomena."

Perhaps they had. However, in the interests of accuracy, I must comment on one point in Mr McEwan's narrative. In discounting the possibility that the sound came from a nearby radio, he says, "The only other building in the vicinity seemed to be a farmhouse, and that was too far away to be a possible source." Obviously he failed to notice the large house that stands next to St Margaret's church, hidden by trees.

That having been said, it still seems strange that no more than a few moments of plainsong should have disturbed the profound silence surrounding the ancient church. Perhaps a phantom choir does sing at St Margaret's from time to time.❦

Three ghosts haunt the Angel Hotel in Lymington High Street.

LYMINGTON

The owners of the Angel Hotel in Lymington High Street proudly point out that it is one of the town's oldest inns. Certainly the building was there in 1675. It was known as the George in those days, not from deference to a sovereign — the first King George came to the throne nearly forty years later — but probably after St George of England.

By 1756 the name had changed to the Angel and Lymington was fast becoming an important coaching station. Stage coaches regularly rattled into the coach house behind the Angel, their occupants seeking refreshment or rooms at the inn while sweating horses were taken to rest and graze at the Nag's Head field. Many a coachman must have lodged at the Angel after a tiring journey over the rough New Forest tracks, which may explain why one of their number still haunts the hotel.

The phantom coachman of the Angel appears very early in the morning, sometimes just as dawn is breaking. Those who have seen the apparition standing by the kitchen window describe it as a shadowy figure which appears to be staring out into the yard. Nobody knows who he was in life, nor why he keeps his dawn vigil.

Another ghost that has appeared on numerous occasions reflects Lymington's long maritime history. Ship-building has been carried on here for centuries. Edward III's invasion army was transported to France in 1345 by a fleet largely constructed at local yards. The town once rivalled Southampton as a port, and merchant vessels used to bring cargoes from all over the world to Lymington. It is hardly surprising that the spectre of a seafaring man haunts the Angel.

Nobody warned a relief manager about this when he moved into the hotel for just two weeks, so he was thoroughly startled by the sudden but brief appearance of a tall, grey-haired apparition at about 11.30 one night. Only when he recounted his experience did he learn that others have often seen this ghostly figure with its distinctive naval coat, brass-buttoned to the neck.

The third ghost of the Angel is said to be a young girl with fair hair falling around her shoulders. Wearing a white dress, she appears on the second floor of the hotel, but nobody knows her story.

An unusual aural haunting was reported by a woman in 1966. Visiting the Angel with her husband, whose brother, a Mr McKinley, was its manager at the time, she left the two men chatting in the bar and retired early to bed on their first night at the hotel. But the constant, irritating noise of a thumping piano prevented her from sleeping.

It came from the old assembly hall adjoining her bedroom, and when Mr McKinley came to say goodnight soon after midnight she remonstrated with him for allowing the disturbance so late at night. The sound had been so clear that she refused to believe the puzzled manager when he told her there was no longer a piano in the assembly hall. Battered beyond repair, it had been taken away to be scrapped just the previous day. And when, at her insistence, the two men immediately unlocked and searched the hall, they found it completely deserted. Had she heard the final performance of a ghostly pianist whose beloved instrument was gone forever?

The Norman church at Boldre, where phantom soldiers have been seen.

The village of Boldre, a few miles to the north of Lymington, is worth visiting to savour the atmospheric peace of its squat-towered church. Work began on this curiously isolated place of worship during the late-eleventh century and nowadays it contains much of interest, including a 1596 'Breeches Bible'. Here too is a poignant memorial to the 1,416 men so tragically lost when HMS *Hood* was destroyed in action against the *Bismarck* in 1941.

But it is the ghosts of earlier warriors which seemingly haunt the ancient building. Opinions vary as to whether the phantom soldiers sometimes seen entering Boldre Church are Normans or Crusaders, while two archers dressed in medieval tunics are reported to have knelt before the altar at dusk with their long-bows at their sides. A Mr Alexander, who once owned nearby Heywood Manor, witnessed the latter apparition.

Back in Lymington, Bywater House has been converted from an elegant riverside mansion into a number of smaller houses. Known as 'Formosa' during the 19th century, originally it was a simple cottage where, it is said, a master mariner — probably also a smuggler — lived during the reign of James II.

A courier's hiding place was unearthed in the garden of haunted Bywater House.

Mr Brodie Munro, whose family has occupied the building almost continuously for some forty years, tells me that visitors and residents often say that they can feel an unusual 'presence' in a room known as The Monk's Room.

Former owners of Bywater House, the Hamilton-Gordon family, were much troubled by supranormal activity after buying it shortly before the turn of the century. The disturbances went on for years. Usually at night but occasionally during the daytime, the footsteps of unseen people were heard moving about the house, sometimes coming up the stairs into bedrooms. Doors mysteriously opened and closed by themselves, noises like the rolling of barrels came from the hall and the family dog was terrified by things only it could see. Guests often enquired at breakfast why their sleep had been disturbed by someone walking about the house.

A remarkable story emerged when a psychic friend revealed to Mrs Hamilton-Gordon through 'automatic writing' that the house was haunted by the troubled spirit of a young man whose mother and sister had been at the court of James II.

Joining Monmouth's rebellion, he was entrusted by the Duke himself after the battle of Sedgemoor with carrying important documents to Holland for safe-keeping; sea transport would be provided by a smuggler who lived at what is now Bywater House.

The young courier stayed at the cottage while awaiting an opportunity to sail for Holland. There he fell foul of the smuggler's daughter Anne, who, to steal his money and jewels, 'prevailed on her lover through jealousy to murder him'. They had hidden his body in 'a well-like hole' in the garden, and now his restless spirit wandered about, searching for the documents that he had failed to deliver. And he wanted Mrs Hamilton-Gordon to help him recover them.

The strange tale revealed by the 'automatic writing' was repeated independently by a medium, who also predicted accurately that the disturbances at Bywater House would diminish with time. Several years later an American medium who examined the writing claimed to see a man in old-fashioned clothes standing by Mrs Hamilton-Gordon.

She secretly took the writing with her when she had her photograph taken in London. When the plate was developed in her presence she was amazed to see, above her portrait, the profile of a fair youth with the distinctive curls of a Cavalier. Then an old lady friend to whom she had shown the photograph had a vivid dream during which the Cavalier took the old lady into the garden of Bywater House in order to point out where his documents had been hidden. Taking a long stick from the summer house, he indicated a spot about three yards away and commanded, "Tell them to dig here."

The Hamilton-Gordons dug where the dream-figure had directed. They found a long paving stone about 18 inches down. It covered a rectangular hiding place, 3 feet deep, 18 inches wide and just under 4 feet long, expertly constructed from narrow, seventeenth-century bricks. The chamber was perfectly dry but quite empty, which came as no surprise to Mrs Hamilton-Gordon. One of her psychic advisers had told her that the avaricious Anne took the courier's money, jewels and documents from the hiding place after killing him.

Discovering his cache seems to have placated the young man's unquiet spirit. Nothing supernatural disturbs today's residents of Bywater House — apart from that persistent, unusual 'presence' in The Monk's Room. As for the smuggler's murderous daughter, it is said that she paid for her sins when the plague carried her off in London. 🖤

NETLEY

Legends are sometimes founded on the flimsiest of suppositions. Such was the case when stories began to circulate about a ghostly woman who haunted the wards of the Royal Victoria Military Hospital at Netley. Some local folk instantly and confidently declared her to be none other than Florence Nightingale. The belief persists, even though it hardly seems likely that her ghost would have had any reason other than morbid curiosity to return there, considering her vehement objections to the design of the place.

Florence persuaded Lord Palmerston to join her in trying to get the plans amended. They were too late. Concerned at the inadequacy of other military hospitals during the Crimean War, the War Office was determined to press ahead urgently with construction of the enormous building overlooking Southampton Water.

Queen Victoria laid the foundation stone and on March 11, 1863, the first patients were admitted to what was then the largest building in the country. By 1870 the hospital catered for 1,400 patients in one-hundred-and-thirty-eight wards. Despite its unsatisfactory layout, the establishment served the country well during the Boer War and both World Wars.

Netley became the main psychiatric hospital for the armed forces in 1950. Already, though, the imposing main building — its corridors on three floors ran for two-hundred yards on either side of the central chapel — was redundant and empty. Fire swept the dilapidated structure in 1963 and three years later it was demolished. Only the Royal Chapel which now serves as the focal point for a country park was saved.

The existence of a ghost at the hospital was once treated almost as a military secret. Staff were forbidden to speak about the phantom Grey Lady who appeared from time to time in a particular corridor or at patients' bedsides, partly because of the Army's understandable reluctance to have their hospital acquire the reputation of being haunted but also in an effort to maintain morale. For it was whispered that a patient was destined to die whenever the ghost appeared.

Stephen Darby, who in the early years of this century recorded numerous Hampshire ghost stories, mentions an early sighting of the Grey Lady by his

The Royal Victoria Hospital's west wing at the time of the hauntings.
(Photo: Parkers, Southampton)

friend Alice Mawcombe. It was around 1878 when she visited her injured brother at the hospital and saw the ghost.

According to Darby's notebook, 'She was dressed in an old-style nurse's uniform of greyish-blue with a white cap and was only a few feet away from Alice. The apparition walked slowly away, making no sound, and disappeared down a passage that led to the chapel'.

Who was the phantom nurse? Darby's researches all those years ago revealed that a nursing sister had committed suicide by jumping from an upper window or from the roof. He maintained that she administered poison to a patient, her lover, after discovering him in the arms of another nurse; overcome with remorse, she leapt to her death. A later variation of the story says that she was distraught after killing a patient with an accidental drug overdose. A third version also has her falling in love with a patient and ending her own life, heartbroken, when he died.

Only the Royal Chapel survived the demolition of the hospital's main building.

Whatever the reason for her death, many reliable people saw her ghost over the years, particularly in the main corridor on the ground floor. A Southampton man who served with the Royal Army Medical Corps never forgot an incident which occurred while he was night orderly on a ward during the summer of 1936.

In the small hours of the morning one of his patients dreamed that he was being choked. Soon afterwards, as he sat making up the patient's records, the orderly experienced a strange sensation, as if time had become suspended. During this dreamlike trance, which lasted two minutes, he saw the spectral Grey Lady pass the door. His patient died exactly four hours later. "I was young and had laughed at stories of the Grey Lady," the orderly recalled, "but not after that morning."

Other members of the nursing staff, hospital officials, patients, visitors — even a priest — also saw the apparition on different occasions. Three night telephone operators often reported sightings. One operator who worked at

Netley for twenty-seven years not only saw the apparition but also heard the swish of a skirt and discerned the smell of perfume after it had passed him.

The 1966 demolition of the building where the ghost walked saw a resurgence of hauntings. Tough workmen were positively terrified by the frequent appearances of an unearthly figure which drifted up and down the stairs, and startled to hear unexplained murmurings in the abandoned wards and corridors.

The demolition contractor himself was in a corridor with four young men one night in October 1966 when they saw an apparition about eight yards away, near a ward entrance. The ghostly woman, seemingly wearing an old-style nurse's uniform, slowly disappeared down a passage. One of the astonished group said later, "The silent figure appeared to be completely unaware of our existence, despite the torches, shouting and noise." That, it seems, was the last reported sighting of the mysterious Grey Lady of Netley hospital. It remains to be seen whether she will appear in the Royal Chapel, the only surviving fragment of the main building.

At the opposite end of the village, the peaceful ruins of Netley Abbey seem the perfect setting for a good old-fashioned haunting. It is easy to imagine, on a moonlit night, the returning shades of those Cistercian monks from Beaulieu who in 1239 chose this spot to build their abbey.

And indeed the resident ghost is said to be that of a monk wearing the white habit of the Cistercians. 'Blind Peter' frequents the abbey cloisters. His task is to guard the fabulous treasure reputedly concealed in a secret passage under the ruins. Brother Peter appears but once a year, on October 31 — All Saints' Eve.

But other apparitions have been reported at Netley Abbey over the years. They are nebulous, unidentified things, strange shapes moving slowly and without apparent purpose through the ruins. Most seem to favour the area around the detached building formerly used as the abbot's lodging, where something disturbing lurks.

David Breeze, custodian of the site on behalf of English Heritage, told me, "A significant number of women of all ages have commented on a feeling of evil in the abbot's lodging. During the past four years, perhaps as many as eighteen individual visitors have gone out of their way to tell me that they didn't

Netley Abbey ruins, their treasure guarded by the ghost of 'Blind Peter'.

like being in there. I don't believe in ghosts, but it seems remarkable that so many people keep saying the same thing."

His scepticism was challenged again by a curious experience on a still, moonlit evening in the autumn of 1991. The custodian's house overlooks the ruins. As Mrs Breeze was putting their youngster to bed at about eight o'clock, she looked across and saw a small, glowing light on top of the abbey. "I went to investigate with my Alsatian dog," David Breeze told me. "I could see the glow clearly as I walked across the lawns." As he entered the abbey ruins he saw that the eerie light was on the high triforium, the raised gallery or walkway above the nave.

It was stationary, about the size of a football, giving off an orange-red incandescence like the glowing embers of a fire. Mr Breeze watched it for a few moments before the glow slowly faded into nothingness.

"Imagine an oil-lamp being turned down," he said. "It was weird, uncanny, but for some reason I didn't feel afraid. My dog was perfectly calm, too. It would have reacted if anyone was there." David Breeze searched the triforium without finding any evidence of intruders or a fire, neither was it a night when one might expect atmospheric phenomena.

Other people have experienced strange happenings at Netley. A motorist whose car engine inexplicably died as he passed the abbey one day saw two amorphous figures moving across from the church towards the ruins. The engine burst into life again as he lifted the bonnet. And a phantom woman dressed in white and carrying a parasol sometimes drifts across the lawns and beneath the elegant arches.

Even the abbey ruins' preservation is due to a remarkable — perhaps supernatural — event. Ownership of the main building, which had been used as a private dwelling for nearly two-hundred years since the Dissolution of the Monasteries, passed in 1719 to a Walter Taylor of Southampton. He decided to demolish it. Many of the ancient stones had already been removed (some were used in the building of a folly, a mock ruin, at Cranbury Park near Otterbourne) when Taylor began to be troubled by nightmares.

He dreamed that a spectral monk warned of dire consequences should he continue the destruction, and that the keystone of a window arch fell and fractured his skull. Friends and acquaintances, notably the father of famous hymn-writer Isaac Watts, advised him against proceeding with the destruction of a sacred building in the light of this clear warning, but Taylor ignored them.

As foretold in the vision, his skull was stove-in when part of the east window arch crashed onto his head. Taylor died, either instantly or, according to another version, when the surgeon's probe penetrated his brain as a stone splinter was being removed. What was then considered as divine intervention put a halt to further demolition.

Another clear warning against tampering with the ruins comes in the tale of a Mr Slown. He decided to search for the abbey's legendary hoard of treasure. Armed with pick and shovel, Slown eventually succeeded in finding the entrance to an underground passage. We will never know what nameless horror drove him from the blackness of his tunnel, screaming in terror and soon to collapse and die of heart failure. But his dying plea has passed into the folklore of Netley Abbey. "In the name of God," he beseeched, "block it up!"

Ellingham Church, where Lady Lisle lies buried near the porch.

RINGWOOD

On the northern outskirts of Ringwood is the village of Ellingham, to where in 1685 a procession of grieving Hampshire folk bore the headless body of Lady Alicia Lisle after her execution at Winchester for treason. The tragic old lady shares a plain, low tomb with her daughter Ann just outside the porch of Ellingham's peaceful little church. But her spirit is not at rest.

Indeed, Lady Lisle seems to have a remarkably active ghost. It has been seen in Winchester's Eclipse Inn (*see* Winchester) and near the church at Dibden on Southampton Water, where in life she often visited her son John. Her head is on her shoulders at Winchester but at Dibden she carries it under one arm in conventional ghostly manner.

She is connected also with the phantom carriage or wagon which appears from time to time, particularly on Midsummer's Eve. Drawn by four headless horses, it rattles along the lane from Ellingham church and across the Salisbury road to Lady Alicia's former home at Moyles Court. No coachman drives the ghastly team, but the lady herself sits inside.

Headless again and on foot, she has been seen drifting through the lonely lanes around Moyles Court. Eerie sounds of carriage and horses have been heard on the drive of the ancient manor house itself. Moyles Court has been used as a school since being sold by the Earl of Normanton in 1962, but for many years previously there were reports of Dame Alice haunting its rooms and passages. The swish of a stiff silken dress and the tapping of high heels were heard as her ghost passed unseen over the bare floorboards. In more recent times, mediums claim to have detected a 'presence' within its walls.

"Dame Alice has been quiet recently," I was told when I visited Moyles Court in 1992. "But there was some strange activity here about four years ago. A number of people commented upon the sudden smell of violets, and once we found that the contents of a locked room had been mysteriously re-arranged."

I also learned about a day in 1962 when the seller's agent showed the empty building to Miss Vesper Hunter, who was seeking a property suitable for conversion into a school. Miss Hunter, who did in fact become headmistress of Moyles Court School, was accompanied on that first visit by her mother. She stayed in the panelled gallery while her daughter toured the building with the agent, telling them upon their return of a woman in black who had joined her as she sat alone in a window seat. This quietly-spoken old woman apparently told Miss Hunter's mother much about the history of Moyles Court, disappearing as mysteriously as she had arrived. The agent confessed himself baffled: he knew that the house was unoccupied . . .

A small property next to the Shopping Centre in Ringwood's Market Place has seen numerous owners come and go over the years. It's an Indian restaurant now, but once it was run as a confectioner's shop by an old lady. Some accounts say she was knocked down by a horse and cart, although people who have lived in Ringwood for many years assure me that the woman — she was Welsh, they say — was killed by a lorry.

Whatever the truth about her death, her ghost was held responsible for haunting the building during 1973. Staff at what was then the Four Seasons restaurant reported classic poltergeist activity. Beer mugs behind the bar began

The ghost of Lady Lisle haunts her former home at Moyles Court.

rattling and swinging on their hooks for no apparent reason, a roll of greaseproof paper spread itself over food on the kitchen table, cutlery moved of its own accord, and so forth. Then the chef was surprised to see 'a lady in long grey clothes' walk past his kitchen door when he was alone in the restaurant early one morning.

"I felt something in the air," he said soon afterwards. "I don't know what it was. I said something like, 'Stop playing around, come on out', but there was nobody there." He left hurriedly after confirming that the building was deserted.

Events came to a dramatic head after closing-time one day when proprietor Peter Hill felt a sudden chill in the air and heard a girl exclaim, "Something's wrong — there's something here!" At that moment a young visitor tumbled down the steep, narrow stairs, knocking himself out. It transpired that he had been startled to see 'an old lady in a grey dress' sitting in a chair at the top of the stairs as he began to come down. No such woman was in the closed restaurant.

Children have seen a ghostly Georgian couple in Ebenezer Lane.

Although a medium confirmed there was 'a presence' within the building, Mr Hill rejected the suggestion of an exorcism. "I won't mind very much if there is a ghost," he said at the time. "After all, it was here before I was."

The idea of an exorcism was similarly repugnant to the owner of a small cottage in Southampton Road. She believed her ghost to be the spirit of a kindly lady, possibly a former owner who still keeps a benign watch over the place. It manifests itself as a peaceful, comforting presence and as an aural haunting. The rustle of a silken dress is heard in the first-floor passage, where an invisible hand softly fumbles with a bedroom door handle.

Another haunted cottage at Ringwood featured in the national press during 1967. It is believed to have stood in Ebenezer Lane since early in the eighteenth century and from the description of their dress its two ghosts also seem to date from that period. The Georgian gentleman and his lady were often seen by the owners' children and by their playmates but, as is so often the case, what was apparent to the young was quite invisible to adults.

The old sign-bracket from which two Roundhead soldiers were hanged.

ROMSEY

A fine example of Hampshire wrought iron work, preserved high on a wall in the Market Place at Romsey, serves as a macabre reminder of a bloody episode during the town's history. It is recorded that in 1642, the first year of the Civil War, two soldiers of Cromwell's army were hung by their necks outside the Swan Inn. Their makeshift gibbet was the inn's ornate sign-bracket.

That much is known. What is open to conjecture is the legend that one of the wretches somehow managed to free himself from the noose and stagger into a narrow alley between nearby buildings. It was but a brief deliverance, because there he died. And to this day some Romsey folk believe that the Roundhead's agonising last moments account for the haunting of premises three doors along from the site of the old Swan Inn.

Matthew Noble's statue of Lord Palmerston stands opposite the haunted restaurant.

Whatever the cause, something unnatural does seem to lurk in the bakery and restaurant known as The Palmerston. Its staff refer to their ghost, not with any great affection, as Charlie. Although he hasn't shown himself for many years, Charlie is said to take the form of a white-haired old man whose haunts — literally — are an upstairs boiler room and the gloomy attic above. One of the waitresses reluctantly agreed to show me as far as the boiler room, but she refused to accompany me through a door and up narrow stairs to the attic. "Charlie's up there," she explained simply.

The manageress, Flo Thorpe, has become accustomed to reports of disturbing events during her sixteen years at The Palmerston. "Many of the staff are afraid to go upstairs and none of us like being here after dark," she told me.

"It's not just the strange noises we hear. Lights switch themselves on and off, and sometimes the toilets flush when nobody is there. Some of us were sitting in the restaurant one evening when there was the most terrific bang from upstairs. We just fled. We never found any reason for the noise."

Equally inexplicable noises were heard in 1977 by a man living in an adjoining flat. Fearing burglars, he called the police to investigate late-night sounds coming from the restaurant. It was like someone using a hammer and chisel, he said. The police officers confessed themselves baffled when, after an exhaustive search, they found the premises empty and no sign of a break-in.

Mrs Thorpe's most alarming personal experience happened on the sad day of Lord Mountbatten's funeral. Some of the police who had been drafted into Romsey for the occasion were taking their meals at The Palmerston. Flo Thorpe was alone upstairs, cooking chips, when she distinctly felt someone touch her on the shoulder. "I whirled round and realised nobody was there," she told me. "I was so frightened, one of the policemen had to come upstairs and stay with me while I did the cooking."

Other members of staff have felt ghostly shoves in the back while working alone. And in 1986 a contract cleaner declared that he would never go back to the restaurant. He had been cleaning inside the building the previous night when the locked back door suddenly crashed open for no apparent cause. The terrified cleaner took to his heels when all the lights began flickering.

Charlie seems to enjoy playing with the lights. During the late 1970s the then manageress, Mrs Ada Mole, often found the lights coming back on again after she had switched them off at the end of the day. Then there were the shopfitters who carried out a major refit of the premises. Working late, they turned off all the lights when they left, but as they climbed into their van they saw that the lights in Charlie's upstairs domain were back on again. The workmen climbed the stairs three times that night to switch the lights off, and on each occasion they had flashed back on by the time the men reached their van. They gave up eventually, leaving the building ablaze with light as they went home.

Some of the odd events at The Palmerston may indicate the need for an electrician and a plumber, rather than an exorcist. The staff, though, have no doubt who is responsible. "He's still up there somewhere," Flo Thorpe told me, raising her eyes towards the attic. ❦

SOUTHAMPTON

The Romans who settled near a bend in the river Itchen early in the first century named their encampment Clausentum. Four-hundred years later they were gone, but reminders of their stay are not confined to the artefacts in Southampton's museums.

Ghostly Roman soldiers, singly or in groups, have long been seen in the area now known as Bitterne Manor, sometimes drifting across the busy main road to the consternation of unwary motorists. The phantom cohorts were particularly active during the period when the new Northam Bridge was being built across the Itchen, and sightings are still reported from time to time.

A retired bank manager who lives in a village to the east of Southampton agreed to give me details of a fairly recent manifestation on the assurance that I would respect his anonymity. Even after eleven years he is anxious to avoid ridicule. "I know what I saw," he said. "I just don't want my name to be associated with it." He used to commute daily between his home and the city centre branch of a major bank, unaware that there were phantoms at Bitterne Manor. Then he met one.

"It was on a Tuesday evening during October 1981," he recalled. "I had left the office at about seven o'clock after working on some urgent papers. As I drove round Bitterne Manor bend a figure moved out from the left-hand side and began to cross the road without stopping. It was about twenty yards in front of my car. At first I thought it was some fool crossing carelessly. Then I realised that the figure somehow appeared to be walking about two feet below the road surface, as though its legs were chopped off at the knees. It was a muddy white colour, not too clear, but I definitely had what I can only describe as an impression that it was an ancient Roman soldier.

"It seemed to be wearing a short, swishing tunic, and something on its head, perhaps a helmet. I saw no weapons or shield. You have to appreciate that it was all over in a brief moment. I was braking instinctively. The figure passed in front of my car and simply dissolved just before reaching the middle of the dual carriageway. I have seen nothing like it before or since. And I promise you I hadn't touched a drop all day!"

The notorious bend at Bitterne Manor, where ghostly Roman soldiers are seen.

The bemused bank manager told only his wife and, next morning, his deputy. "I knew I could confide in him," he said. "He had lived in Southampton all his life and had heard of similar sightings over the years. It was comforting to know that I wasn't the first to see such a thing."

Ghosts from a different era may have been responsible for the strange goings-on at Tatwin Crescent. Even after an exorcism was performed, they continued to trouble the tenants of a block of flats on a sprawling estate of predominantly local authority housing on the city's eastern outskirts. The flats are said to have been built on the site of an old house where a number of paupers perished while camping in the grounds during a particularly severe winter at the end of the nineteenth century. That tragedy seems to be the only clue to the disturbances reported during the early 1970s. They always happened in winter.

A couple were driven to move out of their flat by "the number of things that happened to us." The most alarming event occurred one evening after they

Poltergeist activity and phantoms have been reported in these Tatwin Crescent flats.

returned home to find the baby-sitter trembling with fear because their piano had kept playing, all by itself. Their disbelief was rudely shattered as a "terrible atmosphere" filled the flat and the piano started up again.

Eighteen months later, other tenants recounted their own experiences. One young woman was sitting in her living-room when she heard the front door of her flat open and close. Looking through the glass-panelled door of the living-room, she saw a figure coming down the hall. It disappeared as it reached the door, and when she summoned the courage to check the front door she found it securely locked. The figure appeared again later that night, standing by her bed before vanishing after a few seconds. On another occasion, while she was working in the kitchen, her gas cooker suddenly rocked in several directions, so violently that all the plates rattled.

The ghostly figure of a man also appeared and disappeared on a number of occasions in the hall of her 22-year-old neighbour's home. And another woman became so frightened that eventually she could not bear to be alone in her flat. She regularly found ornaments from the sideboard scattered on the floor in the morning. Moans and heavy breathing followed her around the flat, and a figure once appeared on her balcony. "It just stood there looking at me," she said at the time.

A young couple knew nothing of the disturbances when they moved into a flat with their children. Before long their bathroom taps began to turn themselves full on in the middle of the night, and when the mother tried to turn them off she had the impression that some strange force was preventing her. She had a similar experience some weeks later when the living-room lights suddenly switched off; again, something seemed to stop her from switching them on.

Visiting relatives were startled when a shadowy figure appeared momentarily in the children's room. On another occasion, as the couple sat watching evening television, they distinctly saw a man with his face pressed against the glass panel of their living-room door. Nothing was there when the husband jumped up to investigate. Like the other affected tenants, he found the main door to their flat was properly locked against earthly intruders.

Tragically, the husband was killed in a traffic accident near Basingstoke in August 1973. About three days later his young widow was in their bedroom when a wardrobe door unaccountably swung open and one of his suits flew out, landing on the bed. The distressed woman's comment reflected the feelings of other tenants at the time: "These flats have become a living nightmare".

A long history of hauntings is associated with a restored medieval house in French Street. Dating from about 1290, when wealthy wine merchant John Fortin built it to be both a shop and his family home, the building's basic structure has survived severe damage at the hands of French raiders in 1338 and Luftwaffe bombs in November 1940. It served numerous purposes during the intervening six-hundred years. Divided into three tenements in the seventeenth century, it later reverted to a single building as Mrs Collins's Lodging House for Theatricals.

Various traders came and went over the years. As the Bull's Head Inn by the end of the nineteenth century, the old house already had the reputation of being haunted. It was said that some unseen spirit in the cavernous cellars frequently blew out candles when coal was being collected.

The great-grandparents of Mrs Dorothy O'Beirne from Sholing,

French Street's haunted house, originally the home of a medieval merchant.

Southampton, ran 'the Bull' in those days and her grandmother, Sarah Jane Allen, lived there for a year after marrying their son in 1900. Mrs O'Beirne distinctly remembers her grandmother's story. "Granny, who of course was young then, regularly saw a woman's ghost at the head of her bed as she awoke early in the morning," she told me. "She said it was very visible. Its dress was a dirty white or grey colour, and it would disappear when she tried to wake her husband." Mrs Allen also claimed to have found a tiny baby's skeleton while helping to clear out the cellars.

Increasingly disreputable owners occupied the building during the first half of the present century. Its steady degeneration from seedy boarding-house to common brothel came to an abrupt end when most of French Street was wiped out in a World War II air-raid. But ghostly echoes of its days as a cheap whorehouse survived the bombing.

One of several mediums to have investigated this undoubtedly haunted house decided that the spirit of a man who had committed suicide in an upstairs back room still lingered there. He had suffered from what used to be euphemistically termed a 'social disease'. And tales are told of a prostitute who was battered to death by a seaman after a dispute over the charge for her professional services. She may be the phantom woman who has appeared and as quickly disappeared on several occasions since the end of the last war — although, as we shall see later, there is another candidate.

For more than twenty years from 1950 an amateur theatre group known as the Student Players used the building as their club and rehearsal rooms, scenery store and workshop. They reported many strange happenings.

A shadowy figure — some said it was a woman's ghost — would appear in the upstairs back room and drift through the rear wall, where a bricked-up doorway was later discovered. Footsteps were heard on the wooden staircase, the solid double doors at the front of the house sometimes swung shut of their own accord, and several members of the company were startled to feel something push them from behind on the rickety open landing. There were also occasions when a cold, clammy sensation suddenly filled the air.

All this prompted a few members, one of whom was a medium, to conduct a seance one evening. They later claimed to have made contact with a woman named Ruth Dill, who said that in life she had had a predilection towards stealing jewellery. She admitted killing a sailor for his valuables which, for some unspecified reason, she had thrown down a well.

When someone said he didn't believe a word of it, the table threw itself violently against a wall, making a dent in its plaster. Was Ruth Dill trying to indicate the well's position? The amateur ghost-hunters were greatly excited to discover a circular depression in the path outside the building, immediately opposite the mark where the table had struck the wall. It would be nice to report that this was Ruth's well, and that jewels were found there, but at the time of writing no well has been discovered on the site.

English Heritage undertook an extensive and imaginative restoration project during the early 1980s. I understand that workmen experienced feelings of unease in the old building, particularly in the massive cellar where lights would unaccountably dim or flicker. And often, at about four in the afternoon, they felt a distinct, inexplicable chill pervade the air.❦

Testwood House, where several people have seen the ghost of a tall man.

TOTTON

A phantom woman in the attic, ghostly footsteps, an eerie face at the window of an empty pantry, a laughing male spectre, haunted stairs leading to a forbidding room, a phantom coach — all have been reported at a former royal hunting lodge on the outskirts of Totton.

Tales are told of a murder at Testwood House, perhaps two-hundred years ago. Time has blurred the details but popular belief is that the cook was killed by a manservant who dumped her body in what is now known as Cooks Lane, on the other side of the Salisbury road. Some versions say the murderer was a coachman, others blame the butler or a groom. Another story tells of the butler dying in a back room of the house during a fight with the coachman, his rival for a woman's affections.

Do their ghosts haunt Testwood House? Or are its phantoms the shades of other occupants during its long and chequered history? The oldest parts of the building are believed to date from the fifteenth century, when it was probably a yeoman farmer's house. Later it passed into the ownership of the early Tudor monarchs. Henry VII, Henry VIII and Edward VI are reputed to have used it as a base while hunting in the New Forest.

The Paulet family lived there for some three-hundred years, making extensive alterations and additions which were continued by successive private owners. More recently the house was used as a country club, and from 1958 by sherry importers Williams and Humbert as the offices for their new storage and bottling depot. Testwood Vintners followed. Now they too have gone, leaving the old house and its ghosts to other office workers.

Supranormal activity has been reported at Testwood House for many years. Stephen Darby, an early ghost hunter who kept a journal of Hampshire hauntings around the turn of the century, mentions phantom figures being seen there. A ghostly dog sometimes appeared in the drive, where clattering hooves and rumbling wheels were heard on occasions, as if an invisible coach was rushing up to the house.

In more recent times, the caretaker employed by Williams and Humbert could never persuade his dog to go up a particular flight of stairs. Once, when he tried to force it, the cowering animal turned and bit him. Many staff members and visitors have remarked on a strange, unpleasant atmosphere on those stairs and in the top-floor corridor. They lead towards an attic bedroom where, according to the owners of the country club that formerly occupied the house, a ghostly female figure appeared during the early 1950s. It is said to be the room in which the cook met her death.

Heavy carpets were fitted in all the corridors and rooms during Williams and Humbert's occupancy. Despite this, the sound of footsteps echoing as if on bare boards was heard by several members of staff in areas and circumstances where they could not have been caused by earthly beings.

Their heavy tread startled the caretaker as he checked the building late one night. He was on an upper floor at the time and it sounded as though someone was walking on wooden floorboards along a corridor below. A thorough search confirmed that he was quite alone in the locked building.

Doors at the back of Testwood House rattled violently for no apparent reason.

The apparition of a tall man made its first appearances about a year later, during the winter of 1961. Tales of the hauntings had been kept from the caretaker's son and daughter. As they came up the drive late one night, returning home from a dance, they saw a man at the front door of Testwood House. He was tall, they said later, wearing a long coat and a high hat, and he appeared to be trying to open the door. The figure simply disappeared as they drew closer.

Williams and Humbert's chef saw this phantom man twice in one evening. Working late in his kitchen, he glanced up when he had the impression of being watched. He at first dismissed the tall figure that materialised briefly just a few feet away from him as an hallucination due to fatigue. But he had no such doubt when he saw a man similar in appearance walking towards the front door as he drove away from the house later that night. He got out of his car to challenge the stranger, who was wearing a top hat and a long, caped overcoat or cloak over what appeared to be evening dress. His white shirt was crossed by something in blue and white stripes. As the chef approached, the ghostly figure turned towards him and vanished.

An apparition dressed in similar clothing was seen by another member of staff in broad daylight a few weeks later, at 10.30 am, standing by an entrance gate. A rough sketch made by this worker showed a tall man in a long coat and high hat, with what appeared to be a long, thin chain hanging from his neck.

That drawing assumed special significance three years later when no less a personage than Williams and Humbert's company secretary had an unnerving experience during one of his periodic visits to Totton in January 1965. Based in their London offices, he knew little about the Testwood ghosts and so was content to continue working on his papers in the haunted attic room after staff and cleaners had gone home. A taxi had been ordered to collect him at 7.30 pm and he left the room shortly before that time.

He was annoyed to discover the empty house in complete darkness, leaving him to grope his way along the corridor and down the stairs. And yet later the cleaners emphatically and unanimously denied having switched off the lights when they left. To add to the mystery, the caretaker remembered them being on when he looked across the yard from his cottage at eight o'clock.

The secretary saw an uncanny sight as he descended the main staircase into the hall. The dim light from an outside lamp allowed him to see a man sitting at the reception desk with his back towards him. It was a silent, ghostly figure dressed in top hat and cloak, its head thrown back as if the phantom was laughing out loud.

Even as his mind registered what he was seeing, he became aware of something else. Despite the comfortable warmth of the heated house a bitter chill had invaded him, a cold such as he had never felt before. He later confessed to feeling utter terror, mingled with relief at the sight of his taxi's headlights coming up the drive. Presumably reacting in blind panic, his next recollection was of finding himself seated in the safety of the taxi.

The secretary made a sketch the following day. It shows the phantom figure sitting at the reception desk. Although he had never seen the drawing made some three years previously by the witness who saw the figure at the entrance to Testwood House, there were marked similarities.

An equally alarming incident occurred in November 1962. The caretaker suspected intruders when his dog's frantic barking woke him late one night. Accompanied by his teenage son, he rushed across the yard from their

The pantry window, now glazed, where an eerie face frightened the caretaker's son.

cottage to find the back door of Testwood House rattling violently for no apparent reason. They quickly confirmed that all the doors were locked and then split up to check the windows. There was no sign of a burglary, but the son received a terrible fright when he again reached the back of the house.

He shone his torch onto the window of the kitchen pantry, a small room just a few feet square, and froze in horror. A long, pale face was staring out at him, unmoving, unblinking. It could not have been a reflection, because in those days the unglazed window was covered only with steel security bars and a mesh insect-screen.

The boy later described the phantom head as that of a fairly young man with a light pink complexion and pale grey eyes. Rooted to the spot, he watched it for several moments before it slowly faded away as the caretaker ran up in response to his son's terrified shouts. They found the pantry securely padlocked and empty when they checked inside the house, neither was there any indication that intruders had entered the premises.

Independent investigators have examined the door that rattled so fiercely. It fits tightly. No amount of shaking can make it rattle. Why it should have done so that November night remains a mystery, like so many strange happenings at haunted Testwood House. 🍎

Section Three

THE SOUTH-EAST

CROFTON

Some historians claim that the church of St Edmund the Martyr in the old village of Crofton, between Titchfield and Stubbington, dates from King Alfred's time. Certainly it found a place in the Domesday Book of 1086. The monks of Titchfield Abbey who built it as a Chapel of Ease are reputed to have included a secret tunnel to the adjoining manor house, where they lived.

The ghost of Crofton is one of those ancient monks. His cowled figure has been reported on numerous occasions over the years, drifting around the old village or appearing inside the manor house. The wife of a previous owner lived there for nearly thirty years before its sale for conversion into Crofton Manor Hotel. She has told of a strange feeling encountered within its walls and of the two occasions when her husband, a rear-admiral, saw the phantom monk. It has also appeared to at least one hotel guest. He "nearly shouted the place down" when he awoke at two in the morning to find the monk sitting at the foot of his bed, and refused to occupy that bedroom again.

Crofton and its ghost hit the headlines in October 1978 after work on a road to by-pass the old village disturbed an ancient burial ground. Startled motorists who felt an icy chill in their cars as they passed the church late at night discovered an unwelcome back seat passenger in the form of the hooded monk. He filled their rear view mirrors, head bowed and radiating malevolence.

One terrified man drove furiously in his attempts to get away, but the spectre stayed with him for more than half a mile. "It was like a nightmare," he said at the time. "I nearly crashed." All of which raised speculation about the causes of two fatal and nine serious accidents on that road since the roadworks began.

Two years later, writer Audrey Gray had "a nasty experience I would not care to repeat" in the church porch. As she pulled open the heavy oak door it was suddenly and unaccountably wrenched from her hands, slammed shut as if by

A phantom monk has been seen near the Church of St Edmund the Martyr.

some elemental force. And for a moment she had the awful feeling that she was not alone in the dark porch.

Strange events have been reported also by several workers employed in the fields of Crofton Manor Farm. Footsteps were often heard when no one was there and a pair of heavy gates were seen to open and close themselves on a windless night. But the most bizarre incidents concerned a dairy shed attached to a large barn. The shed shook and rattled violently on several occasions in 1964, sometimes to the accompaniment of a deafening noise. One startled witness likened the sounds to a stick being drawn along the side of the corrugated iron building and a shower of dried peas hitting its roof. It happened late at night and during daylight, each time lasting twenty seconds or longer, and was investigated by sensible, reliable people. No natural explanation could be found — it was just another of Crofton's many ghostly mysteries.

Crofton Manor, where the monk's ghost appeared in a guest's bedroom (see Crofton).

FAREHAM

The ghost of an old man who earned his living by selling newspapers is said to haunt Redlands Lane, a residential street in the west of Fareham. It seems that he was murdered in the lane many years ago for some long-forgotten motive (surely not for the trifling proceeds of his trade?) and his unquiet spirit is drawn back to the scene of his violent death.

It would be intriguing to discover whether he ever wore a tweed coat or actually lived in Redlands Lane. If so, his spectre may have been responsible for driving a sailor and his wife from a house there during 1965. The woman would hear phantom footsteps going downstairs at about 7.15 each morning after her artificer husband had gone to work, and later they began coming up the stairs. One morning the footsteps continued into the bedroom where she lay facing the window. The frightened woman looked around upon feeling a touch on her

Frenchman's Alley, where a phantom soldier from World War I has appeared.

shoulder, to see a tweed-coated man staring down at her, a silent figure that vanished within seconds.

The same ghost appeared before her husband a few nights later, after a tapping noise woke him at about 1.30. Switching on the light, he saw a man in a tweed coat standing in front of the wardrobe. The spectre again dissolved quickly, but the sailor had had enough. He moved into naval quarters and his wife returned to her former home in Croydon.

Another early-morning ghost startled a post office employee that year as he walked to work through Frenchman's Alley near the town's Lower Quay. It was nearly 4.45 am when Jim Martin heard a strange rush of wind behind him and turned to see the apparition of an elderly soldier rising from the ground. He appeared to be a veteran of the First World War, complete with peaked cap and long khaki greatcoat. The phantom rose four feet into the air, legs astride, rifle and bayonet extended at arm's length as if he was charging — or running away — and vanished through an old factory wall.

A youthful ghost was seen in the Roundabout Hotel at Wallington.

The factory is one of several preserved buildings that reflect the Lower Quay's history as part of a busy eighteenth-century port. Some are reputed to have been pressed into service during the Napoleonic wars as a naval hospital and for holding French prisoners, which may account for the supernatural happenings in them when they were used for light industry during the 1970s.

Strange night-time noises and considerable poltergeist activity plagued the workers in Miltall's factory. Tools mysteriously transported themselves from one place to another, electric plugs fell from sockets and the manufacturing director was astonished to see his desk lamp rise into the air, float about and crash to the floor. In Palmer's factory an ethereal figure emerged from a wall, walked through the workshop and vanished.

On the other side of Fareham Creek, the apparition of a boy has been seen in the eighteenth-century Roundabout Hotel. Staff members who came across the fair-haired youth at various times thought he was about twelve years old. He wore an old-fashioned black jacket and buckled black shoes, and was blamed for sudden falls in temperature experienced in a particular room.

Perhaps appropriately, an unwelcome rise in temperature may have put paid to this ghostly guest. I was told that he hasn't been around since his favoured haunting area at the back of the hotel was destroyed by fire about ten years ago. 🍒

GOSPORT

Stand on the Hard at Gosport on a stormy night and you may hear, borne on the wind from the harbour entrance, the eerie clanking of chains. It is the ghost of Jack the Painter, doomed to swing on a gibbet for eternity. Or so they say.

Jack's restless spirit has been frightening the locals for more than two-hundred years. Christened John Aitkin, he is said to have acquired his nickname from being apprenticed to an Edinburgh painter. Jack achieved notoriety in 1776 by deliberately starting a major fire in Portsmouth Dockyard's rope house. Arrested at the Old Raven Inn at Hook, he was sentenced to death at Winchester and hanged from the mainmast of the *Arethusa* at Portsmouth in 1777.

His corpse hung in chains on the beach at Gosport's Blockhouse Point for several years as a grisly warning to other would-be arsonists. Then some sailors stole the skeleton and left it in macabre pledge for a drinking debt at one of the town's numerous pubs. Only his tortured spirit remains, bound forever to Blockhouse Point, rattling in its chains at midnight.

Many of Gosport's other traditional ghosts seem to have been finally laid to rest under redevelopment. The spectral Royal Marine bandboys who used to play bugle and drum around Forton Barracks are no longer heard. Gone, too, is the Napoleonic French naval officer who died on an offshore prison hulk but returned to keep a tryst with his phantom lady near the old burial ground, to the alarm of Royal Marine sentries.

Demolition of the wartime piers from which thousands of troops embarked for the D-Day invasion of France have put paid to the persistent stories of ghostly boots tramping past night-time anglers at Stokes Bay. But Fort Brockhurst still stands, so there is a chance of hearing the whistling sergeant-major who haunts its corridors.

Nearby Frater Lane holds another reminder of the town's military history. After the Dieppe raid and the D-Day landings for which it was such a tragic rehearsal, a former smallpox isolation hospital was pressed into service as a mortuary for soldiers' bodies brought ashore at Hardway. Ghostly happenings at the old hospital, reported by scores of people over at least twenty-five years, may reflect the suffering it has witnessed.

The whistling ghost of a sergeant-major haunts Fort Brockhurst.

Dogs show a marked aversion to entering the building. Murmuring voices, the sound of a chair scraping on the floor and the whiff of curry have all been discerned in empty rooms. On other occasions a shadowy figure has unaccountably drifted past its windows. Heavy weights used by people attending gym classes there have inexplicably moved several feet across the floor.

Something once worked its way along the back of the building, tapping on windows — although overgrown brambles make them impossible to reach. And a number of people were startled to see the shadow of a fully-grown person pass across the floor on a sunless day. None of these alarming events has ever been explained satisfactorily.

Hardway itself was the venue for hauntings reported in January 1984 by a respected Gosport magistrate, the owner of a coach firm with garages in Quay Lane. He heard the story from one of his drivers, who told him that he had seen someone walk silently past the garage office window at about midnight. When the driver rushed out to challenge the supposed intruder, who was wearing a long brown coat and peaked cap, nobody was there. Whatever had passed the window had, quite simply, vanished.

The firm's foreman driver, who had been with them some twenty-six years, then came forward to admit that he had often been unnerved by the identical experience but had been reluctant to say anything previously for fear of looking foolish. The only tentative explanation for the Quay Lane manifestations was that there had been a suicide in an old boathouse nearby many years before.

Another shade from the past scared a pest control officer as he drove home along Wilmott Lane near Anns Hill cemetery in 1991. It was ten o'clock at night when an eerie figure dressed in black cape and top hat emerged from a side road — riding a very old bicycle. The phantom's appearance left the motorist feeling numb and cold, but at least it set his car clock working again for the first time in five months.

A pathway runs northwards from Anns Hill cemetery, between allotments and the back gardens of bungalows. Children and not a few adults avoid it after dark rather than pass a house which stands there, an old white-walled building known to successive generations of imaginative youngsters as 'the haunted house'. A significant number of level-headed people say they have glimpsed figures on that path or in their nearby gardens, shadowy images which disappear as quickly as they are seen.

Typical is the evidence of two practical, down-to-earth women, mother and daughter, whose home adjoins the lane. They have lost count of the occasions on which figures have passed their side window, always singly and usually moving towards their back garden and the old house. "We used to think it was someone coming to visit us," the mother told me. "When we opened the back door nobody was there. It sounds impossible, but they had just disappeared. My husband stopped laughing at us when he had a similar experience.

"I have seen a little old lady scurrying past at least twice, as if she had a mission in life. And a hooded figure has passed the window on several occasions." Similar sightings were reported by a woman living at the other end of her street.

These recurrent spectral appearances do seem to be linked to the area of that old house. Known as The Hermitage, it was built about one-hundred-and-

Apparitions have been seen near The Hermitage, the home of 'Friendly John'.

fifty years ago on the site of a much larger building. There is a strong belief locally that the earlier structure was a monastery. According to some historical notes passed to the owners, it comprised between sixteen and twenty rooms, all on one floor, with a long central room used as a chapel.

The pillars at the back of the present house and the corners of its sitting-room once formed part of the original building. A length of its boundary wall still stands, while areas of mosaic and other remains have been unearthed in the garden. Cellars or tunnels are believed to lie beneath.

Three Catholic brothers and their sister made a home there from about 1730 after fleeing religious persecution in Holland. They lived as virtual hermits, making stained glass in their barn. Sadly, none of the archways, fancy ponds and grottoes which they built in the grounds have survived. The Vigars —whose descendants occupied the house until about 1884—seem to have been gentle people, so it is surprising to learn that one of them was transported to Tasmania for some unspecified crime.

Perhaps his troubled spirit returns to the place where once he found refuge and contentment. Carrie Kentfield, whose husband's family occupied The Hermitage for some seventy years, told me of an intriguing entry found in her father-in-law's diary after his death. 'Whenever I had troubles,' he recorded, 'I would go to the bedroom and Friendly John would tell me what to do'.

Did this kindly wraith also visit Mrs Kentfield while she lived at The Hermitage? It happened at about 5.30 one morning, probably in 1981, as she lay in bed after seeing her husband off to work. "I looked up and saw a man standing in the bedroom doorway," she told me. "He was short, with a ruddy complexion, dressed in black trousers and a black, shiny jacket. His hair was black and swept back, as if it was greased. There was an air of peace about him and I wasn't in the least afraid."

Mrs Kentfield watched the figure move across the landing before deciding she should investigate — in case it wasn't a ghost. But it had disappeared and the house was empty. Five years later a woman who had not heard Mrs Kentfield's story saw an identical ghostly shape at The Hermitage.

The gentle phantoms who go about their business in this quiet corner of Gosport provide no cause for alarm. Certainly there is nothing sinister about the house itself; residents and visitors experience a warm, inviting atmosphere inside. 'Friendly John' has never appeared to the present owners, although Mrs Vicki Pointon tells me that she and her husband often experience the strange feeling that someone is upstairs.

A Gosport ghost that has put in a recent appearance is the woman who haunts Bury House. She has drifted through the corridors and stairways of this fine old mansion, now a community association's headquarters, for many years. A twelve-year-old girl encountered her in 1991. She was a small, bespectacled woman, said the girl, wearing a gown and with her hair in a bun who "just sort of walked straight through me."

Six years earlier a helper was "knocked back a bit" when a strange shape materialised in the kitchen. He described it as a headless, legless body, whitish-grey and moving no faster than walking pace. Other people working with him were astonished to watch the colour drain from his face as he stared towards the apparition only he could see.

Perhaps the answer to the Bury House haunting lies in the strange rites

Bury House — haunted by the ghost of a little old lady.

practised there in Victorian times. Its wealthy owner Thomas South and his daughter Mary Anne were intensely interested in ancient cults and mystic religions. During their tenure, Bury House became the focal point for seances and other serious experiments in mesmerism, spirit communication and alchemy — the secret art of making gold from base metals.

Thomas South was so alarmed at what his daughter wrote in a published book that he went to great expense in recovering all available copies, burning them on a huge bonfire at Bury House. Mary Anne was the ripe old age of ninety-two when she died in Yorkshire. Does her shade return to haunt her former home, or is it one of the unquiet spirits recalled during those bizarre experiments?

Finally from Gosport comes a ghost story as chilling as any told around a blazing Christmas fire. It concerns a house that once stood in King Street, on the site where the Masonic Hall now stands. This house had the reputation of being haunted, which is why at the turn of the century it was offered at a ridiculously low rent to a carpenter who had moved down to work at Camper and Nicholson's boatyard.

Site of the haunted house in King Street, now occupied by a Masonic Hall.

The carpenter and his wife would leave for work early each morning and return late at night. That is when they would hear, drifting around the house, indistinct sounds of children at play, voices alternately laughing or bickering as youngsters will. They assumed them to be a neighbour's children, although they did wonder why they were never seen and why they were not in bed earlier.

The couple bought presents for their relatives on Christmas Eve, returning home with the gift-wrapped parcels. All save one contained presents meant for adults: the exception was a small china doll intended for their grandchild. As they entered the house the air was filled with excited childish voices, an elemental force rushed towards them and icy, unseen fingers eagerly snatched the parcels from their arms. They fled in terror and put up for the night at the nearby Crown Hotel.

On Christmas morning the carpenter returned with some friends, determined to collect his belongings and quit that terrible house. There on the hall floor they found the parcels, torn open and smashed by angry hands. Only the child's doll lay undamaged.

A true story? I do not know. But the late H. T. Rogers, a former Mayor of Gosport, was assured that these strange events actually happened. He researched the King Street haunting and discovered that a woman 'baby farmer' was hanged about a hundred years ago for drowning children in the nearby harbour. And she lived in King Street . . .🍎

A ghostly sailor of Nelson's navy attends St Peter's Church, Northney.

HAYLING ISLAND

St Peter's Church has stood in the north of Hayling Island for more than eight-hundred years, ample time in which to acquire a traditional church ghost. But it boasts no spectral monks or white-shrouded graveyard apparitions. Instead, it is haunted by a phantom sailor.

He is one of Nelson's men, sporting the stiffly-tarred pigtail of the period, and rather lacking in decorum — he wears his straw hat in church. Members of the congregation would see him in the nave or sitting quietly in the back pews, but it seems he has not attended divine service for several years. If he has, no one has reported spotting him at St Peter's.

And what has become of the ghostly railwayman who haunted the island's old station? In May 1990 bulldozers demolished the buildings once associated with the famous Hayling Billy, a little tank locomotive fondly remembered by generations of holiday-makers. It last ran on November 3, 1963,

Old Fleet Manor, where the Man in Black has been seen and sensed.

after which the axed station was used for a while as a local council storage yard before being abandoned.

Henry Cutting of Langstone High Street told me of his dog's strange reaction when he explored the derelict station before its demolition. "I started to go into the ticket office but my dog suddenly refused to budge," he said. "It was scared of something in that building. Its hackles rose and it became quite upset, whining and crying. I tried yanking its lead but it just would not go in. I entered alone eventually and couldn't see anything to make the dog behave like that."

Some years earlier, in March 1969, a workman was kneeling at a job when he sensed someone standing behind him. Glancing round, he clearly saw a pair of trousered legs and black boots which faded away as he jumped to his feet. On another occasion a Havant Council employee was alarmed to feel an unseen hand grab his arm while he worked at his desk.

Ghostly hands of a more soothing nature evidenced themselves at Old

Fleet Manor. One of Hayling's oldest houses (some historians claim it to be the oldest), this fifteenth-century former farmhouse is built of wattle and daub, which can be seen through a glass wall-panel inserted by the late Colonel Lionel Sheppard. He lived there for some seventeen years from 1943, enjoying its old beams, low ceilings, and stairs so narrow and tortuous that the only way to get a coffin downstairs was through a trapdoor or 'coffin-drop'. It is still there, cut into the floor of a large bedroom.

A schoolmistress of one of Colonel Sheppard's sons often slept in that room during the summer holidays. As she lay in bed one night, a phantom hand stroked her brow and she felt fingers running through her hair. "I'll never stop in your house again," the teacher told the family next morning — and she never did. The colonel's daughter-in-law told me the story, adding that he had not been surprised: he and other visitors had felt the soothing hand on their brows on numerous occasions.

"Many strange things happened in that house," she recalled. "Several people saw the ghost of a woman walking down the back stairs. My husband met her once, coming down as he was rushing upstairs. And something used to walk through the sitting-room into the library. Nothing was seen but many people sensed the presence. The dogs would bristle as it passed."

She remembered a Sunday afternoon, at about 3.45, when she waited with Colonel Sheppard's wife for him to come back from shooting. "We heard the back door open, then we saw the door from the long room into the cloakroom also open, and we distinctly sensed someone come into the house. But no one was there. The colonel arrived home about five minutes later."

Sharing his home with a phantom never bothered Colonel Sheppard. "He won't harm you," he would assure the nervous. "It's only the man in black." Both the colonel and his daily help often encountered this ghostly figure dressed in black. It was seen also by several visitors and continued to appear after Colonel Sheppard left Old Fleet Manor. According to psychical researcher Joan Forman, who interviewed the colonel in his new home, the spectre apparently so frightened a domestic employed by his successor, a Captain Illingworth, that she immediately gave notice and left.

A teenage girl, not related to the Sheppards, quietly assured me that she has encountered three ghosts there, although no one will believe her. She once

Aural hauntings and a phantom woman have been reported in the Royal Oak at Langstone.

saw a woman up against her bedroom window; a boy "like a Victorian sweep's lad" appeared in another room; and in an attic-type room at the top of the house she saw "a tall man in black with a sort of goldfish bowl head."

The present owners have occupied Old Fleet Manor for some ten years. The lady of the house tells me that family and friends have experienced nothing unusual, so perhaps Colonel Sheppard's grandson should have the last word. "He was a typical colonel of the old school," he says. "It would not have been in his nature to invent ghost stories."

LANGSTONE

Nobody fully understands why some people see and hear ghosts when others do not. Perhaps their minds are more receptive to supernatural phenomena. Bob Wallace tells me that no phantom has troubled him during more than ten years as landlord of the Royal Oak at Langstone, but it was a different matter during Peter and Joan Spring's thirty-year tenure from 1948.

From their first night in the centuries-old pub they heard footsteps slowly mount the stairs, move along the corridor and stop outside their bedroom. Nobody was there when they investigated. It happened so frequently on subsequent nights that after a while the couple no longer bothered to search the empty corridor. They also learned to live with the sound of chairs scraping on the stone floor of the bar when no customer was there, a very loud sound as if somebody was pushing the chair back to stand up. Their married daughter Penny likened it to the noise made when a chair was pulled across the stone tiles.

But her first fright came when, as a little girl, she awoke to find her bedroom light on. Penny thought it must be her mother, until she saw that the door was closed. Then it opened, closed again, and the light switched itself off.

People and animals have sensed a strange presence in the waterside inn. Joan Spring remembered a businessman who booked in for three nights, only to check out hurriedly the following morning after reporting, ashen-faced, his conviction that somebody or something unseen had entered his room during the night. Her grand-daughter Samantha also stayed only one night in a particular bedroom. The child awoke her mother with hysterical screams, begging to be moved to another room for reasons she could not explain.

Then there was the occasion when some buttons were removed from cardigans and turned up in another room. And something made the family dog, an old spaniel called Tweedledee, abandon her long-established practice of sleeping in the bar.

Rushing downstairs at their pet's frantic midnight howls, Mrs Spring found it in a frenzy of fear, hackles up and barking at some invisible presence. The dog bolted upstairs to cower in the Springs' bedroom. From that night, Tweedledee refused to enter or stay in the bar unless someone was with her.

Langstone Mill, where a holiday visitor saw a boy's ghost.

Whoever or whatever haunts the Royal Oak, only one actual sighting of a ghost has been recorded. Joan Spring saw it in 1969. Her daughter used to sleep-walk, so Mrs Spring was not surprised to be awakened by someone in her bedroom one night. But as she sat up she realised that the white-dressed figure at her bedside was not Penny but an ethereal woman who drifted across the room and faded away through a wall. She never appeared again.

Another spectre that apparently made only one overt visitation was seen nearby in Langstone Mill House. Petersfield artist Flora Twort made her studio in this old cottage alongside the mill, and it was later occupied by marine artist Richard Joicey. Mrs H. M. Ingham, a naval officer's wife who rented part of the cottage from Flora Twort for her family's summer holiday, never forgot the day when she stood in its long larder while clearing away after lunch.

Something, a feeling of presence, made this 'tough, practical woman' turn. A boy was in the larder doorway, a faceless phantom who vanished within seconds, but not before Mrs Ingham had noted his fair hair, white shirt and stockings, brownish-yellow breeches and buckled shoes. Who he might have been, or why he returned to the black cottage overlooking Langstone's peaceful Saltings, nobody knows.

A ghostly monk drifted through a bastion wall at Portchester Castle.

PORTCHESTER

Portchester Castle was nearly a thousand years old when the Normans invaded, and another thousand have since passed. Enough monarchs, monks, fighting men and wretched prisoners have quartered within its walls over the centuries to provide a galaxy of ghosts, yet the splendid ruin traditionally boasts only one. And a disappointingly nebulous phantom it is too. Most witnesses simply refer to 'something tall and white'.

According to legend, a sixteenth-century lady in white appears at the full moon, dragging chains as she seeks the lover who spurned her. Others say the white ghost is a prisoner, fulfilling his vow to return from the grave. Local historian George Crouch poured scorn on these stories in 1979. They spread, he claimed, after a practical joker dressed in a white sheet frightened his friends during the early 1900s.

But other spectres have been seen here. Even after forty-three years, one practical, sensible Portchester woman (she has asked me to identify her only as Brenda) vividly remembers a day when she stood in front of the castle, watching children play hide-and-seek. To her astonishment, the figure of a monk emerged from a small, iron-barred gateway to the left of the main entrance. "He wore a brown, cowled robe," she told me. "The image was so clear I could see the tassels of his corded sash swinging as he walked. He moved along the front of the castle wall and disappeared into the side of the bastion by the main gatehouse."

A former custodian's wife once encountered the ghostly monk in her cottage, which stood immediately outside that gatehouse. And on another occasion, years later, a woman reported that, like Brenda, she too had seen a monk walk along the castle front and vanish into the bastion wall.

Brenda herself became the castle's custodian for twenty-one years. She recalls an assistant custodian, previously sceptical about ghosts, who in 1980 saw what appeared to be a woman bending over a grave by the twelfth-century church that stands well inside the castle grounds. He didn't even wait to turn his car around when the phantom suddenly dissolved before his eyes. Hastily reversing all the way out of the grounds and down the road to Brenda's house in Portchester, he arrived with an urgent plea: "Give me a drink, Brenda — quickly!"

PORTSMOUTH

Local authorities often suspect ulterior motives when tenants complain of hauntings in council-owned homes. Inventing troublesome ghosts can be a ploy towards obtaining alternative accommodation. But clearly this was not the case when a young mother claimed to be sharing her Portsmouth council flat with a spectre named Matthew.

Lorraine Maltby was adamant that she did not want to be moved from her home at Droxford House, a block of flats in Buckland's Alexandra Road. She was happy to be living there. Her family and friends were nearby and she had just finished decorating. She simply wished to be rid of a ghostly co-tenant.

Droxford House was built in 1957, on the site of some old terraced

Tenants have been disturbed by strange events in Droxford House.

houses. Miss Maltby's unnerving experiences began soon after she moved there in November 1987 with her baby daughter Holly. Strange knockings were heard, there were loud noises on the fourth step of the stairs and Holly's toys inexplicably moved. Lorraine Maltby sensed a presence which became 'stronger and braver' as the months passed; at first, a faint shadow would materialise at the top of the staircase but eventually the ghost became so bold it actually climbed into her bed. That was the first and only time she saw it, the figure of a black man in his early 50s with greying hair who held out an arm towards her.

Two council wardens who visited the flat were startled to hear notes from an electric organ, although it had no batteries and was not plugged in. One of them declared he would never set foot in the flat again. Miss Maltby sought help from pastors of two churches. "We wouldn't waste our time if we didn't think she was genuine," said one priest after praying in her flat.

Then she consulted a medium, who told her the spirit's name was Matthew. It was using her psychic potential, he said, and her subconscious was encouraging it. Finally, after she had endured the hauntings for some ten months, a priest performed an exorcism which, one hopes, has put an end to Matthew's visits.

But in February 1990 other paranormal events were reported by tenants living on the second floor of Droxford House. One woman often found her jumper being tugged when she was sitting alone, and her grand-daughter said she had seen the figure of an old man in the bathroom.

Next door, Mrs Cheryl Emm would hear footsteps from upstairs although she was alone in her flat. The stereo door clicked continuously and her fridge-freezer somehow switched itself off twice, although it was impossible for her three-year-old son to reach the plug. A mobile hanging in the boy's room would begin to swing even when the air was perfectly still, and he told his mother that he had seen strange faces in the bathroom. Then Mrs Emm spoke to the previous tenant, who said she was once startled by the appearance of the figure of an old man wearing a grey suit in the bathroom. According to a medium the spirit of a middle-aged man called J. Mullen, whose house had been demolished to make way for Droxford House, was responsible for these visitations.

Much older ghosts, shades from the city's roistering past as a bustling naval port, are said to haunt the defensive rampart known as King's Bastion in Old Portsmouth. Bushy-whiskered sailors and phantom women dressed in grey have been seen here.

Those old salts may have enjoyed their last earthly drink nearby in what was once known as The West India and Quebec Tavern, a white-timbered building which on two sides drops straight into the sea. Built in 1754 as a bathing house, it later became a public house and a hotel. General Wolfe's body was taken there after the battle for Quebec, hence the name. And in May 1845 Captain Alexander Seton of the 11th Dragoons died at The Quebec Hotel from gunshot wounds sustained during the last 'official' duel fought in England, on Gosport's Browndown Common.

It's called Quebec House now. For more than half a century the old house was owned by Pickfords, who used it as a holiday retreat for employees. Marjorie Grimes, who lived there as housekeeper for some twenty years, reported unusual noises and occurrences, some capable of rational explanation but others, such as the radio suddenly switching itself on, which left her baffled. She grew to accept these odd events, saying dismissively, "Captain Seton is walking again."

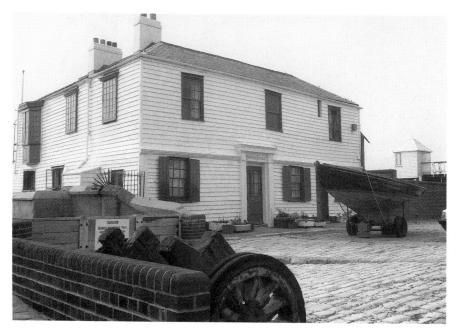

Historic Quebec House, formerly a bathing house and seafront tavern.

On numerous occasions spanning several years, Mrs Grimes saw the clear impression of a man's face appear on the sitting-room ceiling. And one new cleaner hardly crossed the threshold before throwing up her hands, exclaiming that she could sense the house was "full of poltergeists."

Mrs Joan Parker remembers Marjorie Grimes showing her a silver sailing trophy which stood on a chest on the landing. Shaped like a tree, its solid 'branches' slotted into the 'trunk' with pegs nearly two inches long. "It was impossible for those heavy metal branches to fall out by themselves," Mrs Parker told me, "but one of them suddenly jumped out of its slot and landed with a bang on the chest one evening." Joan Parker, who succeeded Mrs Grimes as housekeeper, also recalled how dogs seemed to have an aversion to the lounge during her tenure. Typical was the reaction of a King Charles spaniel owned by a Pickfords' architect. "That little dog could never be persuaded to go into the lounge," she said, "although he was perfectly happy everywhere else in the house."

The Victorian offices in St Michael's Road, haunted by a beadle's ghost.

Pickfords have since sold Quebec House into private ownership. I was keen to discover whether there have been further unusual happenings in this historic building; however, its present owner politely but firmly declined to discuss the subject of ghosts.

More forthcoming were the staff at the Registrar's Office in St Michael's Road. There are three imposing Victorian buildings here, reputedly built on the site of an ancient churchyard. They were once the administrative offices for the workhouse, and one of them still bears its original legend 'Overseer's Office 1879'. The right-hand house, number 1, is said to be haunted by the beadle's ghost, complete with long grey coat, top hat and a carved stick which is occasionally heard tapping on the ground. Number 2, the central building, is now used for the registration of births, marriages and deaths, and it is here that the most recent phenomena have been experienced.

The Registrar's staff are reluctant to enter a certain first-floor room where, they told me, they often feel a distinct, unwelcoming chill. A shadowy figure is sometimes seen, moving silently past the door when no one is in the

A murdered serving wench is the resident ghost at the White Swan.

corridor. It was from this room that a man reputedly flung himself to his death, becoming impaled on the spiked iron railings that once fronted the building. In another room, where the clock has inexplicably run backwards, lights switch themselves back on after being turned off.

An assistant registrar told me of the time when her grandmother, the then caretaker's wife, was startled by the appearance of a spectral man dressed in a black cloak. It was on an upper floor, at a spot where formerly there was direct access into number 1. A cleaner was badly shaken by seeing the identical figure in the same place on a separate occasion.

Not too far away, in Guildhall Walk, the resident ghost at the White Swan is a serving wench who was murdered by her sailor husband during the late 1880s. Customers still report sightings of her wraith, floating past the old fireplace where he committed the dastardly deed. The landlord's nephew swore he saw the apparition of a woman there in 1991.

Next to the White Swan stands the Theatre Royal, a beautiful Victorian

Phantoms have been seen and heard in the Theatre Royal.

theatre being lovingly restored to its former splendour. Theatre historian and stage manager John Offord kindly showed me around, indicating the office where an assistant manager shot himself in 1923 after some unpleasantness over money. But, said Mr Offord, it is not his ghost which haunts the building. That position is filled by an actor who cut his throat in a dressing-room during the 1880s. He now makes unscripted appearances at the back of the theatre, right up in 'the gods'.

Geoffrey Wren, a former general manager, was one of many people who have heard ghostly footsteps in the theatre on numerous occasions, while over the years staff and actors have reported feeling an unseen presence. John Offord was the theatre's barman in 1958, when a startled actress told him of her strange experience. "She had been waiting in the wings," he recalls. "Right on her cue she distinctly felt someone nudge her towards the stage. But no one was there when she looked around."

Also in that year an associate director connected with the resident repertory company was cured of his previous scepticism about the theatre ghost. It was past one o'clock in the morning when Robert Stigwood and a friend agreed to show two young art students the haunted dressing-room.

They knew that the building was otherwise deserted, but as they stood in the somewhat bare dressing-room the lights suddenly went out and the door

Right: The steps in the Theatre Royal where a spectre frightened a guide.

slammed shut. Then, from the corridor outside, they heard what Mr Stigwood described as "angry footsteps" walking up and down.

With some trepidation they opened the door — and found the corridor empty. The four men hastily prepared to leave the theatre, Mr Stigwood switching off the corridor lights, but he had gone hardly six yards before they unaccountably clicked on again. "That really did it!" he told a newspaper reporter. "I don't know what to believe now about the ghost."

Another spirit said to haunt the building is that of Henry Rutley, who managed the old Theatre Royal from 1856. Rutley used to pat employees on the back when praising their work, and long after his death in 1874 cleaners would feel phantom pats as they scrubbed a particular corridor.

And whose ghost frightened the theatre's chief guide in October 1984? This eminently sensible woman, who has asked me not to reveal her name, says of her experience: "It's something that will stay with me forever." She even remembers the precise time, 10.15 on a Saturday morning. Climbing the gloomy backstage stairs towards the director's office, head bent to see the darkened steps, she sensed someone coming downstairs. "I actually stepped aside to let him pass," she told me. "He was two steps above me. He had surprised me, making me jump, and as I looked up I said, 'So sorry, you startled me'.

"The figure appeared absolutely real and solid," she continued. "He was about six-foot-two-inches tall, very thin, wearing a long cloak — like an old coachman's cloak, with a shoulder cape — and a wide-brimmed hat with a flat crown. I didn't feel threatened in any way whatsoever. But as I looked at him, he began to fade away until I could see right through him: he was dematerialising. I turned tail and ran when I realised what I had seen."

Let us leave Portsmouth on a lighter note, with the chords of a haunted piano. Mike Frewing, landlord of the Connaught Arms in Fratton, thought he had a bargain when he bought the second-hand instrument in 1987. But on its first night in the bar, he and his wife were awoken by the furious barking of their two Rottweilers. Fearing intruders, Mr Frewing took the dogs into the bar, where they ran towards the piano, snarling angrily at it for no apparent reason. The Frewings' slumbers were again disturbed on another occasion by the sound of phantom hands playing the piano in the middle of the night. They promptly sold it, ghost and all, and slept soundly thereafter.❦

A phantom horseman has appeared in the woods behind the Old Rectory.

ROWLANDS CASTLE

Ghosts were the furthest thing from her mind as the rector's wife walked her dog through the woods near her Rowlands Castle home one December day. Mrs Forse was more concerned with gathering sufficient ivy and other evergreens to decorate their church for the forthcoming Christmas celebrations. Then she saw a motionless rider on horseback in the near distance, not too far away for her to note his long fawn coat or cloak.

She looked away for some reason, only briefly, but during that moment horse and rider mysteriously disappeared. And when Mrs Forse investigated she discovered the area was so overgrown with thick brambles, bushes and dense undergrowth that it would have been impossible for any horseman to have been there. At the same time her dog made it very clear that he had no wish to pass the spot. Stopping dead in his tracks, he began trembling, obviously distressed and unwilling to go on.

Charlie Pearce's ghost walked this path in front of the church.

The animal needed no second urging when his puzzled mistress told him to go home. He immediately turned and bolted away. "When I got home I found him waiting at the back door of the rectory, still shaking like a leaf," she recalled. The dog behaved in a similar frightened manner when they again reached the overgrown area some months later.

That ethereal rider who haunts Gipsies Clump — part of Havant Forest — is the ghost of Charlie Pearce, a colourful character who occupied a cottage at Rowlands Castle during the nineteenth century. Some accounts say he was a poacher, others claim he turned to thieving and highway robbery to finance his drinking. For Charlie was a drunkard whose favourite companion was a black kettle full of gin. It was to prove the death of him.

Drunk beyond care, Charlie set off on horseback through the woods one day. He probably didn't even notice the overhanging branch that caught him by the throat, pulled him from his horse and broke his windpipe. But his ghost returns periodically to haunt the very woods where the rector's wife met a phantom horseman.

Miss Daisy Baker, who taught at the village school for some fifty years, often saw Charlie's ghost at Gipsies Clump. More frequently, though, she would see it walking or riding from the direction of the Old Rectory and down the path past the church, vanishing as it reached her school. She sometimes came quite close to the silent apparition, vainly trying to converse with it. It was then, said the teacher, that she noticed livid weals where the throttling branch had bruised Charlie Pearce's throat. 🐛

WARBLINGTON

Little remains of the ancient village of Warblington, down among the flat fields at the head of Langstone Harbour. The flint-walled church of St Thomas-a-Becket is still there, dozing away the centuries. Its peaceful churchyard is guarded by two grave-watchers' huts, grim reminders of a time when body-snatchers came at dead of night to rob fresh graves of their corpses.

And there are the ruins of Warblington Castle, a fortified house built in the early-sixteenth century for Margaret, Countess of Salisbury. She was not destined to end her days in this once-splendid building. Instead, her opposition to Henry VIII during the turbulent intrigues of the Reformation led her to the Tower of London and the executioner's block in 1541. Margaret Pole went out in a dreadful manner, chased around the scaffold while refusing to kneel for the fatal blow. "These grey hairs know no treason," she declared defiantly. Then a bungling axeman incompetently hacked off her head.

The Parliamentarians destroyed Margaret's castle in 1644. Only a solitary gatehouse tower still stands, just along the lane from the church. But the countess returns from time to time, headless of course. Dressed in a white burial shroud, she drifts about the lanes near her castle ruins, through the lonely churchyard and across nearby fields.

A Havant railway porter swore he saw her ghost one night while walking home past Church Lane, which leads to the ruins. It was a shadowy white vision, said Mr Fradgley, steadily groping its way along the hedge. With tingling scalp, he ran hundreds of yards before calming down.

On another night a bus driver and his conductor were taking their empty

Margaret Pole's ghost is said to haunt the lanes around Warblington church

vehicle from Havant to Emsworth at the end of a tour of duty. The dual carriageway had not been built then, so they were using the old road. As they passed Warblington both men clearly saw a figure emerge from the south side and move slowly across the road. Thinking it was an intended passenger the driver stopped his bus, but the apparition simply disappeared.

The Countess of Salisbury might encounter other phantoms on her nocturnal wanderings. According to tradition a ghostly smuggler who was killed in a quarrel and now roams the castle ruins is just one of several spectres haunting Warblington.

The area abounds with ghost stories. Even its quaintly-named Pook Lane was known for years as Spook Lane, and I have spoken to locals who still take their children ghost-hunting there. But undoubtedly many of the old stories were invented to frighten inquisitive villagers away from the smugglers' trails that led across the flat coastal plain from secret landing places around Langstone Harbour.

One of those paths would have taken the smugglers along Pook Lane, past Warblington parsonage. It has gone now, replaced during the eighteenth century by a building known today as the Old Rectory, but the original parsonage was the venue for a haunting so celebrated in the annals of the supernatural that it is worth describing in detail here.

Warblington parsonage stood empty through the autumn and into the winter of 1695. Even when the rector, the Reverend Richard Brereton, despairingly offered the considerable inducement of a £10 reduction on the annual rent, no villager could be persuaded to take up the tenancy. They remembered how the last occupants had hastily packed and fled in terror with their child and servants.

Brereton's curate, the young Reverend Thomas Wilkins, knew from personal experience what had driven Thomas Perce and his wife from the house. Anxious to find new tenants, Brereton urged him to say nothing, but on December 15, 1695, Wilkins was persuaded to make a sworn deposition about the alarming events at the parsonage.

His remarkable testimony is made more compelling with the knowledge that he was an educated man, Bachelor of Arts of some six years' standing at Oxford's Trinity College and a man of whose behaviour 'no ill report' was heard. As to stories of apparitions, he said he was previously 'an infidel'. He did not believe in ghosts.

The hauntings, said Wilkins, began on a Monday night, towards the beginning of August 1695. Thomas Perce, his wife and their manservant (also named Thomas) had gone to bed at about nine or ten o'clock, leaving the maid to rake up the downstairs kitchen fire. As she turned from this chore, a candle in one hand and the Perces' child in the other arm, she saw a black-gowned figure walk through the room and out of the door towards the orchard.

Her screams brought the Perces rushing downstairs. The maid was so distraught that 'she would not that night tarry in the house, but removed to another belonging to one Henry Salter, farmer, where she cried out all the night from the terror she was in, and could not be persuaded to go to the parsonage house upon any terms'.

Mrs Perce was sufficiently alarmed to consult next morning with the Reverend Wilkins at his Havant lodgings. Someone, perhaps rector Brereton, was playing tricks, he soothed. But he kindly spent that Tuesday night in the parsonage kitchen with Perce and the manservant, after shrewdly searching the house 'to see if anybody were hid there to impose on me'. He even recited an exorcism to placate the worried tenants.

Wilkins also stayed there the following Thursday, sleeping in the same room as Perce. Next morning he angrily accused the other of deceit when Perce claimed to have seen 'something walk along in a black gown and place itself against a window' before walking off. Perce explained that he had not roused Wilkins because he was too frightened to either move or speak.

Nothing happened on the Friday or Saturday nights when the two men again shared the room. But Wilkins slept alone on the Sunday, with Perce and his manservant sharing a bed in the adjoining room. No doubt the level-headed curate again thought he was being taken for a ride when he was roused, sometime between twelve and two, by alarmed shouts from next door. It was the servant, urging him to come in because something was moving about the room. And it was *whistling*.

He learned later that Thomas, lying in the curtained bed, had heard something walking at the foot of the bed 'and whistling very well' before parting the curtain and looking at the two men for a while. Then it moved away and the frightened manservant shouted for Wilkins.

The curate's detailed testimony records how he called back, asking whether Thomas could strike a light. When he said he could not, Wilkins leapt from his bed and rushed to the other room. Finding it locked, he called for Thomas to open the door. The terrified manservant sprang across the room, unlocked the door and shot back into bed. Wilkins entered the moonlit room . . . and saw the ghostly figure of a man.

He recalled later: 'The apparition seemed to have a morning gown of a darkish colour, no hat nor cap, short black hair, a thin, meagre visage of a pale swarthy colour, seemed to be of about forty-five or fifty years old, the eyes half-shut, the arms hanging down, the hands visible beneath the sleeves, of a middle stature'. Wilkins took scarcely three or four paces into the room before the spectre moved from the bedside and stopped against the partition wall. He boldly approached within an arm's length and demanded to know, in the name of God, what it was that made it come disturbing them.

There was no answer. Thinking it might be someone playing the fool, Wilkins reached out to touch the phantom but 'my hand seemingly went through the body of it and felt no manner of substance till it came to the wall. Then I drew back my hand and still it was in the same place.

'Till now,' he went on, 'I had not the least fear and even now I had very little. Then I adjured it to tell me what it was'. With that, the ghost backed gently along the wall before turning through the door into the gallery or corridor, followed by Wilkins. It disappeared before reaching the stairs at the end of the gallery, although there was no place it could have turned off, leaving the brave curate feeling very cold 'from my feet as high as my middle'. He spent the rest of that night in bed between Perce and Thomas, who complained about how cold he felt!

When Wilkins related his ghostly encounter to the rector of Havant, John Lardner, and to a Major Battin of Langstone, both said the description fitted a former rector of Warblington who 'had been dead above twenty years'. He had been a disgrace to his cloth, a man reputed to have fathered his maid's illegitimate children before murdering them. The original documents identify this errant rector simply as 'Mr P', but tradition supposes him to have been the Reverend Sebastian Pitfield, who used to whistle tunes as he went about the parish.

This was enough for Thomas Perce and his wife. They hastily gave up their tenancy of the parsonage, which remained silent and empty.

But the ghost still walked. On 'the Monday after Michaelmas' — presumably the end of September — a man from Chodson in Warwickshire passed the parsonage while returning from Havant fair at about nine or ten at night. Perhaps he had heard about the haunting, because he decided to investigate when he saw lights in most of the rooms. Peering through the kitchen window, he saw only a light; but as he turned away he saw 'the appearance of a man in a long gown'. Pursued by the phantom, he fled across several acres of glebe and meadow until he was relieved to find a number of men in a barn belonging to the farmer, Henry Salter.

According to Wilkins' statement, 'This man went into the barn, told them how he was frightened and followed from the parsonage by an apparition, which they might see standing against the pales if they went out. They went out,

The Old Rectory in Pook Lane — once known as Spook Lane.

saw it scratch against the pales and make a hideous noise. It stood there some time and then disappeared. Their description agreed with what I saw. This account I had from the man himself who it followed and also the farmer's men'.

We do not know whether the ghost ever put in another appearance. History simply leaves us with Thomas Wilkins's intriguing testimony, sworn before a Mr Caswell and sent with a covering letter to the learned Dr Bentley at the home of the Bishop of Worcester. But there are still those who believe that the area around The Old Rectory (now converted into flats) in Pook Lane is haunted by the wraith of the whistling rector.

And there is a modern footnote to the tale. Pointing out that Sebastian Pitfield died in 1686, only nine years before the hauntings, Mr Michael Pitfield believes his ancestor has been blamed unfairly. His research indicates that Sebastian was not a lecherous murderer and he suggests the Reverend John Payne, rector from 1630 to 1658, as an alternative culprit. Perhaps the major obstacle to this attempt at historical rehabilitation is that nobody knows whether Payne enjoyed whistling.🌱

Ferndale was built across a long-established cattle drovers' trail.

WATERLOOVILLE

Waterlooville has developed from a small village named Waterloo to become part of the suburban sprawl spreading northwards and eastwards from Portsmouth. In Victorian times this was an area of forests and woodland, interspersed with farms and splendid country estates. Today, they lie buried under acres of asphalt, brickwork and small, trim gardens. But the ghosts of yesteryear still return from time to time, as evidenced by two remarkable Waterlooville hauntings.

Ferndale is one of those new roads, a pleasant, wide avenue lined with attractive homes built in the late 1950s. One of them is occupied by a couple who have asked me not to reveal their name; let us call them Mr and Mrs Sawyer.

Somebody once described Mrs Sawyer as 'a typical school ma'am', an epithet she finds amusing but which will serve as an indication of her character. This is no woman given to wild imaginings, but a sensible, no-nonsense person.

When she says that she has seen a ghost in her garden, not once but on numerous occasions spanning nearly twenty years, you have to believe her.

The Sawyers' house happens to have been built across the path of an old woodland track. It can still be discerned in their back garden, where the lawn grass grows darker and more lush along the lines where wooden wagon wheels once rumbled. The couple have taken pains, in laying out the garden, to include a path following that long-established route.

Mrs Sawyer first saw her ghost on a beautifully sunny May morning. She thinks it was during 1975. "I was hoovering the dining-room," she told me, "when I had the strange feeling that someone was watching me. The patio doors were open and when I looked into the garden I saw a man standing in the middle of the lawn, right where the old track used to run. He appeared to be absolutely solid, as real as you are."

The stranger was wearing trousers and what Mrs Sawyer initially took to be a long raincoat but later realised was like a rustic's smock. On his head was a large, crumpled hat — similar to an Australian bushwhacker's hat.

"At first I took him for a prowler," she said. "But, to my surprise, he simply disappeared as I watched. Oddly enough, although I realised that he must have been a ghost, I wasn't in the least afraid. There was nothing scary about him, no feeling of evil, just an overwhelming impression of sadness."

Wondering whose phantom he could have been, Mrs Sawyer took the opportunity of questioning her butcher's roundsman when he called at the house. He was an old countryman, the son of the cook at Leigh Park House, with a wealth of local knowledge. Without telling him the reason, she asked if anything tragic or unusual had happened in the area.

"He immediately told me about a suicide which occurred about a hundred years ago," she said. "He had heard the story from his father. A cattle drover used to drive his beasts along our old track, from Hambledon to the market at Havant. One day he disappeared; his cattle were found wandering along the track without him. When the woods were searched, they found him hanging from an oak tree."

The roundsman was not surprised when Mrs Sawyer now told him what she had seen. He pointed out that developers had recently felled a number of old trees while clearing nearby woods for the new Hulbert Road. One of them, he

The garden in Ferndale where a drover's ghost has appeared for nearly 20 years.

suggested, was the drover's hanging tree, and his spirit had been disturbed.

Mrs Sawyer has seen the ghost in her garden on several occasions since that first manifestation. He stands there, unmoving, quite distinct at times but at others just a grey form. She has tried to speak to him but he vanishes whenever she approaches. Sometimes he simply makes his presence felt as an otherwise inexplicable cold patch, without being seen. He has a distinctive smell, too — the aroma of rough, old-fashioned pipe tobacco. Mrs Sawyer's daughter sometimes smells the tobacco and feels a ghostly presence, although she has never seen the drover.

And always he is accompanied by an overwhelming aura of sadness. "It is most noticeable," says Mrs Sawyer. "The sad atmosphere persists even after he has gone. There is definitely nothing evil or frightening about him."

She has approached the Hampshire Records Office, to learn more about the event which seems to bind the apparition to that old track. Interestingly, their research shows that a man *was* found hanging from a tree in the area in 1872 but the cause of death — suicide or a lynching— was never discovered.

Mrs Sawyer lives at peace with her benign, melancholy drover. But a totally different spirit, a creature of obsessive malice, was involved in the other local case — the haunting at Hopfield.

Hopfield House stands in a Waterlooville back street, entirely out of character with the post-war and modern homes that over the years have crept up almost to its walls. Oppressive and gloomy, the Gothic building looms over them like something from a Hitchcock film set. It is easy to imagine the strange and dreadful events which happened under its roof.

The mansion — originally called simply 'Hopfield' — was not always so forbidding. Edward Fawkes had it built in three acres of former hop fields sometime during the middle of the last century; certainly he was living there in 1875. His great-granddaughter, Helen McFarlane, has described her childhood memories of its beautiful grounds, tennis court and rose gardens, and of splendid parties on the croquet lawn during the early 1900s.

Hopfield was a family house, intended by great-grandfather Fawkes to be occupied only by his descendants. Things began to go wrong when ten-year-old Helen McFarlane's parents broke that tradition and moved down to Southsea to be near better schools for their children.

The retired couple to whom Hopfield was let on a three-year lease settled in happily enough but before long they received disturbing reminders that they were not of Edward Fawkes's lineage. In anxious telephone calls to Helen's father they described how the old man's spirit had appeared, angrily telling them they had no right to be in the house. Most worrying were the spectre's threats of violence unless they moved out immediately, warning that there would be no peace for anyone living at Hopfield who was not a Fawkes.

The tenants endured his persistently malevolent hauntings for just a few months more before deciding it was impossible to stay in the house. A middle-aged widow took over the remainder of the lease and moved in with her daughter, a woman in her twenties.

We do not know whether the ghost of Edward Fawkes appeared to the women but certainly misfortune overtook them. Although of good health and seeming perfectly well when she retired one night, the widow was found dead in her bed next morning.

Edward Fawkes's descendants were becoming worried. Could he really be exerting an evil influence there? But, despite their concern, they now ignored his wishes entirely: seizing an opportunity, they sold Hopfield in October 1912. And so the house passed completely out of the hands of the Fawkes family.

The new owner, Captain Norman Ernest Playfair, moved in with his wife Mabel in January 1913. At about this time the house was re-named 'The Grange' — a development possibly destined to outrage the spirit even further.

Captain Playfair was a retired military man who had served with the Egyptian Army and the Egyptian Slave Department before being appointed Governor of Suakim. This formerly active man found time weighing heavily during retirement, and during a year at The Grange he became increasingly depressed and mentally unbalanced.

We can only speculate whether the influence of Edward Fawkes contributed to his depression and eventual death. Most accounts claim that he was stabbed in the back during an unsolved murder. But the truth is perhaps even more horrific. My researches confirm that in the early hours of Wednesday March 11, 1914, still in evening dress after dinner, Captain Norman Playfair went into the hall and committed suicide by plunging an ornamental double-edged dagger into his left chest. His wife, who had been in the cloakroom, rushed out and caught him as he fell dying.

According to Mrs Sheila White, to whose account I owe much of what follows, this tragic death and the previous events caused the house to remain unoccupied until the end of the 1920s, avoided by the locals who dubbed it 'The Haunted Grange'. Then the dilapidated mansion passed into the hands of Mr Roger Whitaker Nowell, a wealthy Purbrook man with whom Sheila White's family were friends.

She has described how her father and others were appalled by the palpably evil, forbidding atmosphere of the grey old house. They begged Nowell not to buy it. But he did so, spending lavishly to extend and restore it into a glorious showpiece — and he again named it 'Hopfield'.

But the house seemed to defy all the thought and money expended to turn it into a happy home. I have before me the reminiscences of a good friend of the Nowell family, someone who made many visits to them at Hopfield and yet was always grateful to leave its "very unpleasant influence". Some forty

Hopfield, about 1910 — before the hauntings began.
(Photo: courtesy Hampshire Museum Service)

years later the writer still remembered it as a grey, menacing building.

Sheila White shared this opinion. She described Hopfield as a "great, grey, dour house". And she certainly had good cause to remember her family's first visit to the restored building as Christmas guests of the Nowells.

Barely fourteen years old and alone with her little dog Scraggie in an isolated bedroom, Sheila was awakened by her pet growling in its basket. Sitting up in the pitch blackness, she was astonished to receive a sharp crack on the head, accompanied by a dreadful sensation of encasement — as if she had been buried alive. Then she realised that for the first (and last) time in her life she was inexplicably lying *underneath* her bed.

She groped her way out and found the bedside light switch. As light flooded the room she found Scraggie crouched in a corner, staring at the door with hackles raised, snarling angrily. Then she saw the handle turn and the door slowly opened. No one was there. Sobbing with fright, Sheila seized the dog and fled to her parents' room.

She never slept in that room again. Each night, without telling their hosts, Sheila's father occupied her bed while she slept with her mother. He always felt a presence in there, as though he was not alone. And each night, no matter how tightly or how often he closed the door, there came a moment when its handle turned and it swung slowly open.

Then it seemed that the curse of Edward Fawkes had struck

Hopfield House today: haunted by memories of a spiteful spirit and violent death.

again. Roger Nowell's only son, a personable young man with a brilliant brain and clearly destined to enjoy a bright future, came to Hopfield from university to spend his first vacation with his parents since they had moved into the house. Unaccountably, this talented young man took himself into the basement one evening, pointed a shotgun at his head and killed himself.

A few years later, broken by her son's tragic suicide, Mrs Nowell died at the house. Soon afterwards, in November 1938, Roger Nowell himself collapsed and died in his dressing room. He was survived only by their daughter Evelyn, who soon moved out of that terrible house.

Again abandoned, Hopfield lay empty for many years, neglected, overgrown and decaying. Few people would have wished to make their home in a haunted house with such a reputation for tragic death. Eventually the Royal Marine Orphanage occupied the building for a while during the war, before it was converted into eleven flats.

They call it Hopfield House now. It retains an overwhelming air of greyness, the same atmosphere of quiet malevolence experienced by Sheila White and others all those years ago. The big front door sags on its hinges and from a gloomy hall the staircase leads upwards into uninviting darkness. I was not sorry to leave that brooding house and its memories of Edward Fawkes.❦

BIBLIOGRAPHY & FURTHER READING

ALEXANDER, Marc *Haunted Inns* (1973) and *Haunted Churches and Abbeys of Britain* (1978)

BARDENS, Dennis *Ghosts and Hauntings* (1965)

BEDDINGTON, Winifred & CHRISTY, Elsa *It Happened in Hampshire* (1937)

BOASE, Wendy *The Folklore of Hampshire and the Isle of Wight* (1976)

BRODE, Anthony *The Hampshire Village Book* (1980) and *Haunted Hampshire* (1981)

BROOKS, J. A. *Britain's Haunted Heritage* (1990)

CHALLACOMBE, Jessie *Jottings from a Farnborough Notebook* (1922)

COPE, Joan *Bramshill* (1938)

COXE, Anthony *Haunted Britain* (1973)

CHILCOTT-MONK, J. P. *Ghosts of South Hampshire and Beyond* (1980)

FORMAN, Joan *The Haunted South* (1978)

GREEN, Andrew *Our Haunted Kingdom* (1973)

GUTTRIDGE, Roger *Ten Dorset Mysteries* (1989)

HALLAM, Jack *The Haunted Inns of England* (1972) and *The Ghosts' Who's Who* (1977)

HARRIES, John *The Ghost Hunter's Road Book* (1974)

HERBERT, W. B. *Railway Ghosts* (1985)

HOLE, Christina *Haunted England* (1940)

JOICEY, Richard *Langstone — A Mill in a Million* (1976)

McEWAN, Graham *Haunted Churches of England* (1989)

O'DELL, Noreen *Portrait of Hampshire* (1979)

PERKINS, W. Frank *Boldre* (1927)

PLAYFAIR, Guy *The Haunted Pub Guide* (1985)

POOLE, Keith *Ghosts of Wessex* (1976) and *Unfamiliar Spirits* (1989)

ROBBINS, Rossell *The Encyclopedia of Witchcraft and Demonology* (1959)

UNDERWOOD, Peter *Ghosts of Hampshire and the I.o.W.* (1983) and *This Haunted Isle* (1983)

WHITAKER, Terence *England's Ghostly Heritage* (1989)

WILSON, Colin *Mysteries* (1978)

Also — *Hampshire: the County Magazine*; *Hampshire Chronicle*; *The News*; *Southern Evening Echo*; *West Sussex Gazette*.

INDEX

PUBLISHER'S NOTE

We hope you have enjoyed this tour of Hampshire's haunted places. It has been written and published in a genuine attempt to explore, and in some measure explain, the phenomena we usually refer to as hauntings. Certainly it has not been published to encourage anyone to delve into the darker corners of 'ghost hunting', and on a purely practical level we would request that you do not disturb the people living in any of the properties mentioned or pictured in this book or trespass on private property.

As much of the material in this book was volunteered by people the author met on his travels it would appear that a great many 'ordinary' people do have much to recount on matters supernatural. It is also apparent that there is a great deal of interest in this subject. With this in mind we are now planning to produce a second volume on Hampshire's haunted places and would welcome information and experiences in written form, from people who feel they have a story to tell. Any such submissions will be treated in the strictest confidence as to source but the substance of the submission may be used in a future publication. Please write to us at: Ensign Publications, 2 Redcar Street, Southampton SO1 5LL.

Hampshire PLACE·NAMES

RICHARD COATES

NEW BOOK — HAMPSHIRE PLACE-NAMES

Arranged alphabetically, with over 850 entries, *Hampshire Place-Names* provides extensive information on the names of towns and suburbs, villages and hamlets, manors and parishes and rivers and forests in the county. Drawing on the most recent scholarship, and with a wealth of detail, the book explores the formation and development of each place-name.

Hampshire boundaries have changed somewhat from the nineteenth century onwards but Richard Coates includes all the places in Berkshire, Dorset and Sussex that used to belong to Hampshire.

A fascinating introduction tells the linguistic history of the county and shows how place-name evidence can reveal some of the darker corners of English history. Cultural, geographical and topographical factors are taken into account to establish the original form and meaning of each name.

Each entry includes a range of spellings dating from around 1100 to the present day, a suggested translation of the name together with a full discussion of the alternatives and interesting misinterpretations put forward over the years.

As the first comprehensive book devoted to this subject, *Hampshire Place-Names* will delight local historians and place-name enthusiasts alike.

THE AUTHOR — HAMPSHIRE PLACE-NAMES

Richard Coates has taught linguistics at the University of Sussex since 1972. He is a member of the Linguistics Association of Great Britain and the Council for Name Studies in Great Britain and Ireland. Author of *Toponymic Topics* and *The Ancient and Modern Names of the Channel Islands*, he has also written numerous articles and papers on linguistics and name studies.

For further details write to us at: Ensign Publications, 2 Redcar Street, Southampton SO1 5LL.

OTHER RECENT BOOKS FROM Ensign Publications

The Story of BITTERNE PARK	£7·95
BOURNEMOUTH THEN & NOW — A Pictorial Past	£12·95
The BOVINGTON TANK COLLECTION	£14·95
BRANNON'S SOUTHAMPTON — The Port & Town	£8·95
DORSET — Customs, Curiosities and Country Lore	£6·95
DORSET MURDERS	£6·95
DORSET PLACE-NAMES — Their Origins and Meanings	£4·95
The LANDSCAPES of DORSET	£14·95
An Illustrated HISTORY of FAREHAM	£12·95
FAST BOATS & FLYING BOATS — The British Power Boat Co.	£14·95
The FOLK SONGS of OLD HAMPSHIRE	£2·95
HAMPSHIRE MURDERS	£6·95
HERITAGE in DORSET and the NEW FOREST	£7·50
LYMINGTON — A Pictorial Past	£7·50
PETERSFIELD — A Pictorial Past	£6·95
A Photographic History of PORTSMOUTH	£14·95
A Picture of SALISBURY	£1·99
A Picture of WINCHESTER	£1·99
A PORTRAIT OF PORTSEA — 1840-1940	£11·95
PUB WALKS in the NEW FOREST	£4·99

PUB WALKS around PORTSMOUTH	£4·99
PUB WALKS around SOUTHAMPTON	£4·99
PUB WALKS around WINCHESTER	£4·99
PURBECK SHOP — A Stoneworker's Story of Stone	£10·95
ROADS AND RAILS around the SOLENT	£13·95
SOUTHAMPTON CASTLE	£2·00
SOUTHAMPTON PEOPLE — Eminent Sotonians and Characters	£5·95
The STORY OF GOSPORT	£9·95
A Study in SOUTHSEA — Arthur Conan Doyle	£10·95
SUSSEX — Customs, Curiosities and Country Lore	£7·50
SUSSEX MURDERS	£6·95
TEN DORSET MYSTERIES — True Tales from the County	£6·95
The TIDE MILL at ELING	£2·50
TITCHFIELD — A Place in History	£5·95
A WALK THROUGH LYMINGTON	£7·95
WATERSIDE — A Pictorial Past	£7·50
The Strange Death of KING WILLIAM RUFUS	£4·95
The WINCHESTER GUIDEBOOK	£2·50

All our books should be available from local bookshops in the area, but in case of difficulty ring 0703-702639 to order any of these books.